Children in the
Second World War

To my children
Eleonore and Eloise

Children in the Second World War

Memories from the Home Front

Amanda Herbert-Davies

First published in Great Britain in 2017 by
PEN AND SWORD HISTORY
an imprint of
Pen and Sword Books Ltd
47 Church Street
Barnsley
South Yorkshire S70 2AS

Copyright © Amanda Herbert-Davies, 2017

ISBN 978 1 47389 356 6

Printed and bound in Malta
by Gutenberg Press Ltd

Typeset in Times New Roman by
CHIC GRAPHICS

Pen & Sword Books Ltd incorporates the imprints of Pen & Sword
Archaeology, Atlas, Aviation, Battleground, Discovery,
Family History, History, Maritime, Military, Naval, Politics, Railways,
Select, Social History, Transport, True Crime, Claymore Press,
Frontline Books, Leo Cooper, Praetorian Press, Remember When,
Seaforth Publishing and Wharncliffe.

For a complete list of Pen and Sword titles please contact
Pen and Sword Books Limited
47 Church Street, Barnsley, South Yorkshire, S70 2AS, England
E-mail: enquiries@pen-and-sword.co.uk
Website: www.pen-and-sword.co.uk

Contents

List of Plates

A twelve-year-old girl helping to dig a trench for air raid protection in Kent, 1939. *(D. Rice)*

A 'homely' Anderson shelter. *(P. Tollworthy)*

A sketch of her family's Anderson by Christine Widger, aged twelve, drawn while sitting in the shelter during a doodlebug attack.

A brick surface shelter built at the bottom of a garden in Kingsmead Avenue, Tolworth, Surrey. *(E. Gardener)*

Evacuee's label. *(W. Hayle)*

Phyl Jones, privately evacuated from East London with her siblings for the duration of the war.

Muriel Booth, aged eleven, who was evacuated on a Thames paddle steamer.

Muriel Booth's plea to come home from evacuation.

Kitty Levey (right) and her sister, CORB evacuees, ready to depart from Lancashire to South Africa.

Jo Veale from Birmingham who was convinced she was 'going home on Monday'. She did not return home for six years.

Christine Widger, evacuated from Kent to Lancashire, kept in touch with her Lancashire teacher for the next fifty-seven years.

Yorkshire boy Ernest Tate, spy-watcher and unofficial member of Leeds ARP.

Daphne Hackett, aged eleven, whose family befriended prisoners from Thames Ditton POW Camp.

German prisoners at Long Ditton POW Camp, Greenwood Road, Thames Ditton, Surrey. October 1946. *(Iain Leggatt)*

Dorinda Simmonds of Ealing, London, black-market butter girl.

Derek Clark's school, semi-demolished overnight by a doodlebug in 1944.

A little boy in Kent playing with his father's ARP kit. *(M. Jones)*

Iain Leggatt playing war games, 1942.

LIST OF PLATES

Alan Starling (left), underage member of the 3rd Battalion Renfrewshire Home Guard, Scotland.

Geoff Creece, GPO messenger boy in Portishead during the Bristol Blitz.

John Bones in uniform as Flight Sergeant in No. 308 Squadron Air Training Corps, Colchester.

Joyce Garvey (1942), who helped a mother give birth in an air-raid shelter, member of Birmingham ARP from the age of sixteen.

Jean Wilson, member of Friern Barnet Girls Training Corps, London.

Jean Wilson wearing her St John Ambulance cadet uniform.

Myfanwy Khan with her older sisters in the garden of her home in Exeter.

The ruins of Myfanwy Khan's home after the Exeter blitz, 1942.

Margaret Hofman, whose family fled the docklands of London during the Blitz.

Sketch of a doodlebug by Jeff Nicholls who was an industrial spotter in London for the Alarm within the Alert.

John Pincham (left) and his brother at home in Wimbledon Park the year before they were bombed-out.

Bomb-damaged houses in John Pincham's street, 1944, which had to be guarded from looters.

VE Day street party in Rothsay Road, Gosport. *(M. Brien)*

Introduction

During the Second World War, Britain was a war zone. Over 60,000 civilians died on the Home Front due to enemy action, millions of homes were damaged or destroyed, and mass migration was necessary to save the vulnerable. The last generation able to give a living testimony of life in Britain during this, one of the country's most tumultuous periods in history, are those who were children. On the Home Front, war pervaded every aspect of life. As a consequence, children from the very young to teenagers were inextricably involved in the war effort and even warfare itself. There was no child who was not, to a greater or lesser degree, untouched by the exceptional conditions of the time.

This book describes the Home Front from the children's perspective, focusing on those experiences which left the deepest impressions. From the cataclysmic wail of the first air-raid siren to the Victory bonfires that scarred the backstreets, these recollections present a comprehensive picture of childhood in Britain throughout the Second World War, as remembered by those who lived it. The experiences of these children who came from all over the country, from every class, are as diverse as the individuals who tell them.

For some children, particularly the younger ones, the war did not detract from a happy childhood because, to them, war was normal. Though conscious of what was going on, they did not have the deeper concerns their parents had. Protected by the optimism of youth which believes tragedy is a lifetime away and dying is for the old, young children were free to find excitement and thrills in war. The fear felt during bombing raids was, as described by one boy, like being on a rollercoaster ride: it belonged to the moment and then it was over; until the next time. Some of these children even considered their wartime childhood to have been an exciting journey, one which did not last long enough. The popular picture of children on the Home Front presents a childhood like this, one which shows children's attraction

INTRODUCTION

towards and the ability to cope with the conditions of war. This is verified by the overall impression of children's experiences which, even when set within the context of war, is one of the cheerful optimism of youth, that ability of children to find adventure and enjoyment in the world around them. The war, with all its restrictions, provided plenty of opportunity for that.

Whether living in the battleground of a Birmingham housing estate or the war-torn tenements of Glasgow, children adapted to war. Gas-mask fitting, a trial that no child could escape, evolved into gas-mask couture with fancy designer cases; the blackout, so intrusive in the lives of adults, gave the freedom of unsupervised play. By day, school lessons were undertaken in semi-derelict schools, greenhouses and tin sheds, while nights were spent in the wartime bedrooms of underground shelters, crypts and caves. Shelter-run etiquette, secret butter runs and auditory bomb-tracking were part of daily life. From spy catching missions to running business ventures with the local POWs, children embraced life on the Home Front. Even that which was designed to cause terror – aerial bombardment –- provided inspiration for creative enterprises: bomb craters made for speedways; shrapnel became the new playground currency; home-made explosives were produced in backyard sheds. There was also the opportunity for direct involvement in civil defence, positions which gave responsibility and pride. Child messengers sped through bombed cities at night, young firefighters stood guard on the top of seven-storey mills during air raids, and underage boys patrolled the parish armed with only the vicar's First World War pistol.

The nostalgia of a time when childhood was defined by war is apparent, yet it is extraordinary considering the circumstances. This was a period in history when it was normal to see aeroplanes falling from the sky, to sit in fear underground night upon night, and to know that people were dying at home or in foreign fields. Families made suicide pacts, children were sent away to be raised by strangers, rockets and missiles flew overhead, and the names of the dead were read out in school assemblies. Explosions, guns, bombs, armed soldiers, fire and death: all were everyday occurrences in a country at war.

CHILDREN IN THE SECOND WORLD WAR

For some war veteran children, the portrayal of the 'good' war does not fit with their experience, and no picture of the Home Front would be complete without including their stories. The children who remained in danger zones under heavy bombardment lived a life where tragedy was never far away: a young boy, the sole survivor, carried out of the rubble of his home; a girl fleeing the burning docklands of London; the bombed-out, destitute and homeless seeking sanctuary with nothing left but the clothes they stood up in. For them, the war took them on a different journey where the fear was never over. Another major source of trauma was evacuation. While some child evacuees were fortunate enough to have a positive experience which resulted in happy memories and life-long bonds, many had a difficult time. Separation, isolation, and struggling with culture shock and social divisions define their wartime experiences. For these children, Britain's child survivors of war, catastrophic events created psychological and physiological problems, family rifts and painful memories. Their voices give a testimony as to the other side of the Home Front – the stark reality of growing up in war. *Children in the Second World War* reveals a childhood of extremes: the excitement and adventure of living during a unique period in British history, and also the fear and terror that war can bring.

Over 200 personal accounts have been used in the making of this book to give a comprehensive, vivid picture of exactly what it was like to grow up on Britain's Home Front. The main source used is the Home Front archives of the Second World War Experience Centre. The Centre is dedicated to the collection and preservation of memoirs, interviews, photographs and other memorabilia from the Second World War. It holds an extensive collection of material from many thousands of individuals and as such presents a major source of historical research. I owe a debt of gratitude to the Centre for allowing me access to their collections, and in particular to Robert Fleming, Company Director and Chairman, for giving kind permission to use text and images from the Home Front archives. I have been fortunate enough to be involved with the Centre over the last five years, and it is from reading the hundreds of files in the Home Front archives that I have been inspired to tell the story of children in the Second World War.

Chapter 1

The Beginning

'We are now at war' – hearing those terrifying words I ran into my bedroom and burst into tears. I was 10 years old.

E. Aynsley

When the Prime Minister's voice echoed from the wireless on the morning of 3 September 1939, the words he spoke changed everything. The broadcast had not been unexpected, but as the Declaration of War reverberated throughout homes all across the country on that Sunday morning it left intense emotions in its wake. From shock and fear to exhilaration and anticipation, no one was unaffected. The day Britain went to war was a day never to be forgotten.

Thelma's mother had been visibly anxious at the recent events in Eastern Europe. The fate of her neighbour's seven sons who she grew up with, all of whom fought in the Great War, was always on her mind; only one son returned home, disabled by shell shock. Now Britain was once again at war. As they sat listening to the wireless that morning, the devastation on her mother's face sent twelve-year-old Thelma rushing outside. She fully expected to see war right there on her doorstep with soldiers marching down the road. Much to her relief, her street in Birmingham seemed to be as quiet as normal; nothing terrible had happened, nothing had changed. She closed the front door with relief, unaware that just over one year later most of that street would be reduced to rubble, obliterated by a landmine that would take the lives of many.

Across Britain, similar scenes were being played out in many households on the morning war was declared. In London, the tension in Richard's house was tangible. He sat at the table diligently completing a jigsaw while his parents snatched whispered conversations. Though he was too young at barely ten years old to fully comprehend the wider reasons for his parent's anxiety, Richard understood that there was now going to be a war and that this must be the reason Mother was crying a lot and cuddling him more than usual. He was oblivious to the fact that his parents were planning to immediately send him away, a decision which would soon leave him feeling as if his whole world had been shattered.

The announcement of war left one family in Blackburn, Lancashire, in mourning. The parents understood that momentous changes were ahead, but at that time they could not yet conceive that war would take their children away on a journey of thousands of miles from which they would not return for six years. A nine-year-old boy in Essex hunched on the stairs with his arms hugged tight around his legs, listening to the sounds of his mother and great aunt crying downstairs as they recalled the Great War, and one ten-year-old fled upstairs when she heard the news and flung herself down on her bed to cry inconsolably. She knew what war meant, she had heard all about her uncle who had been wounded, gassed and temporarily blinded before being sent back to the Front only to be killed: 'War was cruel, it was pain, suffering, death and sorrow, and so I sobbed.'

There was hope. Some people were confident that the war was, and would remain, far away in foreign fields, and others believed it would be over within weeks. In Patricia's home in Twickenham, her father, who had lost a leg at Mons during the last war, reassured his family as he confidently told them that war would not affect people at home. An eight-year-old boy in Lancashire overheard his father and neighbour discussing the news with an air of certain authority: '. . . it will be over before Christmas.' No one could predict that this new war would go on even longer the last one. Teenager Joan cried, afraid that her father would to go to war, but he placated her with optimistic words, convinced that six weeks would be all it would take to sort it out. He would never have believed that five years later their home would be bomb-blasted shell, his daughter a Canadian war bride, and the war would still not be over.

The declaration of war was not bad news for all. For those children who were keen for adventure, this is what they had been waiting for. Bristol boy Donald, nearly seven years old, had heard the news in the cathedral quiet of his grandmother's parlour and had been filled with trepidation: 'My imagination worked overtime – bombs, fighting in the streets, people being killed the very next day.' But he came home to a completely different atmosphere in his street where the local boys were running around wildly in great excitement, leaping in the air and shouting with elation. In Scotland a teenage boy listened to the announcement of war from the parson in church and was barely able to contain his exhilaration while all around him the congregation collapsed in tears. Another eager boy, an eight-year-old in London, ran out of his house to dash down the road so he could start the war straight away by helping to fill sandbags at the newly-erected Air Raid Precautions (ARP) post. His older brother, upset and flustered because he had been at work and so therefore had missed the actual announcement, belted up the street on his butcher's bike to don his Territorial Army uniform and get into the action before it all started without him.

From anxiety, thrill and enthusiasm, children's reactions to the beginning of war ran a gauntlet of emotions, and this included plain indifference. One twelve-year-old schoolgirl treated the news of war as inconsequential. All that tedious adult talk had little influence on her. Her experience of war was long drawn-out history lessons and dry, dusty tomes of books with endless dates. To her, wars were just 'words on a page' and left little impression. That would change. One day she would be the one writing about war – of hiding in a metal cage at night as aerial landmines exploded overhead and her hometown blazed with raging fires; a war that came to life in the blitzing of Britain's towns and cities.

After the Prime Minister's broadcast, a thirteen-year-old boy in Colchester stood in his garden and looked up into the perfect blue sky, wondering what far-reaching changes might lie ahead. There was barely a breath of wind on that late summer afternoon and it hardly seemed the sort of day for such a momentous occasion, the first day of war. In the distance he heard a wailing sound, a rising and falling crescendo of noise that was to become the harbinger of destruction. This was the first air-raid warning of the war.

My Mother anxiously ordered us to hurry home and fill the bath with water in case of a gas attack! No-one in the family ever discovered what this was intended to achieve!

Frank Andrews

It was anticipated that the declaration of war would immediately be followed by an enemy attack, therefore when the first air-raid sirens wailed across the country shortly after the Prime Minister's speech, there was panic. Mothers immediately switched off gas ovens, which ruined many Sunday dinners, or hurriedly filled baths with water in case of gas attacks. Holidaymakers cut short their vacations, frantically packing and fleeing home. People in public places were ushered indoors to places of safety, and children fled home to pull on their gas masks and crouch in the broom cupboard under the stairs with the promise of sweets. Ten-year-old William in South Ealing, London, was one of those running down the street in fright. A few minutes earlier he had been engrossed in watching his best friend's father chase a rat through his cabbage patch with a spade, but then the siren howled. That cataclysmic noise chased him home until he burst through his front door to the safety of his equally terrified mother.

In Stockwell, another ten-year-old was praying she would not die as she crouched fearfully with her mother beneath planks of wood in a timber yard where they had taken shelter when the first sirens wailed over London. She was convinced this was The End as 'school rumours said that we would all be killed in the first air raid'. All across the country, sirens gave voice to the beginning of the war. One nine-year-old girl had been enjoying the novel spectacle of evacuees disembarking at Woking railway station until her mother arrived: 'She was breathless and flustered, in fact in a great panic. War had been declared, she told us gasping out the words in her breathlessness, and there was an air raid on. We must rush home as quickly as we could. The Germans would start dropping gas bombs on us at any minute . . . We were hustled along at breakneck speed with my mother casting fearful glances up at the sky all the way in case those expected German bombers with their fatal load of gas bombs appeared.'

When the first siren wailed over the promenade at Littlehampton it came as a fearful shock to the holidaymakers. There was instant pandemonium: '. . . all hell broke loose, the sirens started blasting, Air Raid Precaution wardens were dashing along the promenade, sounding rattles and blowing bugles, telling everyone to get back home and indoors straight away. It was real panic!' Eleven-year-old Jack and his little sister abandoned their sandcastles and bolted home as fast as they could. Their anxious parents swept them inside and promptly closed all the windows and bolted the doors. After a while, when nothing seemed to have happened, curtains twitched, doors opened and people tentatively stepped outside. Urgent air-raid wardens sped back down the streets on their bikes, shouting orders and wielding rattles, to send them all scurrying back indoors again. Wardens were also busy in London. One boy watched mesmerised as an enthusiastic ARP warden flew down the street on his bicycle wearing a sandwich board painted with the words 'AIR RAID': 'He pedalled furiously along the street and up the hill blowing his whistle as loud as he could. Ten minutes later he repeated the performance in the opposite direction but with "ALL CLEAR" on his signs.'

Indeed, nothing happened; at least, there was no bombing, no gas attacks, no fighting in the streets. In fact, 'the rest of the day for us children passed like any other Sunday' and 'life carried on as normal'. Donald, who had fully expected bloodshed and death, felt bemused as 'nothing seemed different'. However, the day that war was declared would become an abiding, life-long memory for a lot of children, in particular for that first and unforgettable wail of an air-raid siren, the effect of which was summed up by one young boy: '. . . it certainly made the first sixty minutes of war something for me to remember.'

CHILDREN IN THE SECOND WORLD WAR

'They're coming, they're coming and will drop from the sky to gas us and we will all die!'

Dorothy Knopp

The fear of gas was experienced not only by soldiers and war veteran adults, but by children on the Home Front. Horror stories abounded and newspapers and billboards broadcasted dire warnings. Sheena was terrified of what would happen: 'I had somehow got it into my head that "when war broke out" the sky would immediately darken and cloud over with a sulphurous yellow pall and we would all have to live in murk and gloom.' After reading a newspaper billboard emblazoned with an alarming headline warning of imminent gas attack, eight-year-old Dorothy fled home in fear for her life. Gordon, a little boy in Shipley, West Yorkshire, gallantly tried to save his toys by spending an afternoon 'attempting to seal some of my Hornby Railway items in their boxes, to protect them from gas, using sticky paper tape'.[1] Evacuated to his Auntie Dolly's village, Colin found himself sat miserably on a chair in the middle of the night during his first air raid. The grown-ups around him discussed whether to hang wet blankets over the doors and windows in case gas bombs were dropped. Colin knew what mustard gas could do because of his father suffered from life-long disability due to a mustard gas attack on his unit in Belgium during the Great War. Colin felt frightened, sitting there thinking he might die or suffer gas poisoning. He never made it to school the following morning; he was sick after breakfast and remained ill for three days.

Anti-gas measures in Britain had begun well before war was declared. Huge quantities of gas masks were produced, with civilian gas mask production reaching an estimated 107 million from 1937 to 1942. The problem, as most children discovered, was that gas protection was almost as frightening as a gas attack. The introduction to the 'evil smelling, sinister black rubber mask', those terrifying-looking contraptions, became a wartime rite of passage that no child could escape.

A ten-year-old in London found her gas mask absolutely

suffocating: 'I was very nervous of wearing my gas mask, I thought I couldn't breathe properly, so my Auntie sealed up one room with tape in case of a gas attack.' Dorothy, with her fear of gas, now had to muster up the courage to overcome her fear of the mask: 'First the face settled in the mould. Then the straps were tightened over the head so that they wouldn't twist. Any rubber tucked in under the chin had to be eased out. Panic struck as the window steamed up and breathing became a frightening task.' Likewise, ten-year-old Susan found the mask unpleasant as 'the rubber stuck wetly to one's forehead, neck and cheeks, the visor steamed up within seconds, it was impossible to speak or hear properly, and very nearly impossible to breathe.'

Many children took a complete aversion to their gas mask and so did some adults. In Kent, Yvonne's grandmother refused to accept a gas mask. She patted the curlers pinned firmly beneath her hairnet and primly declared, 'I ent gooing to have me net torn . . . if they start flinging gas about . . . I shall goo down the field and put me head in the pond.' One boy's mother had equally strong feelings about her gas mask: '. . . there was no way anyone could get my Mam to put one on.'

Gas-mask practice became a regular part of the school curriculum. It was not a lesson that was particularly enjoyed. Clive's school in Birmingham provided an incentive for getting the infants to put on their gas masks. A sweet was tucked into their gas-mask boxes with strict instructions that it could only be eaten whilst wearing the mask. Clive, with that distracting sweet burning a hole in his gas mask, was given the important duty of gas-warning monitor. This involved 'watching a board sited outside the classroom which had been painted with something that changed colour in the event of a gas attack'. His qualification for this 'very responsible job' for an infant was the fact that his desk happened to be nearest the window. Some schools took gas training a step further and practised extreme education in their very own static gas chambers, while others relied on a visit from the travelling gas van.

The purpose of gas vans and chambers was to educate school children in the value and effectiveness of gas masks by exposing them to tear gas. One little girl, newly evacuated from the East End of London to the outskirts of Wales, took part in this event: 'Not long after we arrived in the village, we were all issued with gas masks which had to be carried with us at all times. In order to impress upon us the importance of this, a sort of mobile gas chamber was situated outside the school gates through which we would be made to walk, first with and then without wearing our masks. The effect that this had on us, when going through the chamber without our gas masks, was to cause our eyes and nose to stream with water, so much so that we were more than pleased to get out of there as quickly as possible.' A primary school boy evacuated to Surrey had to undergo a similar experience: 'One day we had to have our gas masks tested. We put them on and went into a van that was parked in the playground, a dozen or so at a time. The van was filled with tear gas and after a couple of minutes we were let out. If the gas masks were OK, one was alright; if not, the child came out with tears streaming down their face and coughing and spluttering.' One girl panicked and tore off her mask in the gas chamber. 'No teacher or any other adult was in the van with us.' She was so badly affected by gas that she had to be taken home.

As well as gas masks and drills, people were encouraged to take measures to gas-proof their homes and shelters by taping up cracks and gaps around doors and windows to prevent the entry of gas. In Wimbledon, John's father, who had fought in the trenches of the Great War, meticulously sealed up every gap around the doors, floors and walls to create a safe room. This offered greater psychological than physical protection as it was impossible to completely gas-proof old brick buildings, but some people did believe it was possible to make a room completely airtight. At the house of one eight-year-old boy in Eastbourne the family had 'created a Gas Proof Room by sealing the doors and windows'. Unfortunately they became uneasy about a potential problem in their impermeable safety room: '. . . if gas could not enter, neither could air, leading to death by asphyxiation rather than gas poisoning; so we did not use it.'

Gas-mask holders quickly became a fashion statement to show off the latest trends in haute couture, and the 'glamour girls had extra special gas mask cases; designer would be the label we would use today to describe these'. The original container, a plain and uninspiring cardboard box on a string, could be turned into a stylish handbag by purchasing an up-market holder such as one Plymouth teenager's 'pretty imitation snakeskin container' which became 'like a second handbag as it had to be carried around always'. For Sheena in Glasgow, the designer gas-mask boxes were a girls' dream and 'to own a red leather number shaped like a Roses chocolate box was the summit of my seven-year-old wish list'. A little girl in Scotland was 'immensely proud' of her gas mask holder made from 'a pattern in *Women's Own* for a smart gas-mask-shaped holder for your mask, in leatherette or American cloth'. Philip preferred the more robust and boy-friendly containers sold at Woolworths which 'did a roaring trade with metal canisters, like big cocoa tins into which the gas mask fitted snugly and these were much more durable. The disadvantage was that if the tin was dented you could not get the gas mask out and you had to ask someone to get it back into shape for you.' Sheena also liked the tin boxes as they were 'so handy for hitting your friends with'.

While children accessorised their gas-mask holders, homes all across Britain prepared for war by covering windows and doors, drawing curtains, and removing light bulbs. On the streets the lights extinguished, shop windows darkened, and vehicle lights dimmed. Darkness was to descend upon Britain. This was the blackout.

A beneficial offshoot of the ever-changing situation in which we found ourselves, and which was no part of the German planning, was the extra fun youngsters derived from the blackout.

Charles Tyrrell

The blackout was a system of defence which relied on complete co-operation of the community as everyone was responsible for completely blacking out their homes. Not a single light was allowed to be seen outdoors between specified hours unless it was partly obscured, dimmed and pointing downwards. Trial blackouts prior to the war got off to a shaky start. Air-raid wardens in East Yorkshire and Lincolnshire protested strongly when issued with 2,000 German hurricane lamps, and an attempt to blackout the Midlands in July 1939 failed spectacularly when Leicester City Council declined to take part and their railways blazed a trail of light throughout the county.[2]

Preparing the house for nightly blackout could not be approached casually. Curtains had to be closed before lights were switched on, and lights switched off before outside doors opened. The strict blackout regulations meant being very cautious even when performing simple tasks like putting out the bins. Eight-year-old Basil's house in Essex had a regime for emptying rubbish into the outside bin at night, a task which had to be executed with military precision: '. . . for some reason the inside kitchen door would be closed first, the light turned off before opening the outside door. You then had to find the dustbin. You couldn't simply make a quick dash. A knock on the door and wait until you were told it was alright to come back in.' Also in Essex, a six-year-old girl was diligently 'trained never to put a light on until I had first closed the curtains. This habit became so ingrained in me that I have continued to do it all my adult life.' In desperation to comply with the blackout regulations, some families preferred to remove light bulbs than take the risk of revealing a glimmer of light. In Kings Heath, little Gwyneth sat in the bath in the dark. Her mother, afraid of having a warden knocking on the door, had taken the precaution of confiscating the bathroom light bulb.

In Basil's house they exchanged their bulbs for low-wattage ones and even the toilet had the dimmest of bulbs, a 25-watt. In Canning Town, London, the neighbour of a ten-year-old boy had the optimistic idea of dimming all the light bulbs in his house by painting them black, '. . . but all he got for his trouble was ridicule from his family as they stumbled about in almost complete darkness, not to mention the smell of burning paint whenever he put the light on'. Those homes with gaslight turned down the wicks and 'Blind Man's Buff was the name of the game, as you moved about your house after dark, unless you carried a small torch or a shaded candle'.

Failure to follow the blackout regulations could make the offender liable for three months imprisonment or a hefty fine, such was the serious nature of the crime. An accusation of flouting the blackout resulted in one farmer threatening litigation on the local community in Buxton, Derbyshire, where ten-year-old Laurence lived. A random, off-loaded bomb had landed near a farmhouse but the farmer was blamed for attracting the bomber by showing a light: 'The farmer became so exasperated with these nasty rumours that he had to place an advert in the local paper saying that he would sue anyone else propagating this scurrilous story!' On one occasion, an entire community flouted the rules and staged a blackout rebellion. A strange event that happened one night in Durham brought nearly an entire village out in the streets to watch, including young Vincent: 'There, we joined all our neighbours, gazing up at the incredible sight of hundreds of magnesium flares descending gently on parachutes and Langley Park was lit up as though it was day. We could see clearly the whole length of our back street with little groups of people all along it engaged in animated discussion. In fact virtually the whole village turned out that brilliant night and speculated as to the meaning of it all but, of course, no one could shed any (extra) light on the matter and mostly we just enjoyed the spectacle.' The local ARP wardens were outraged at the mutinous displays of light from open doors and windows and frantically tried to usher people indoors, but nobody took the slightest bit of notice. Considering the circumstances, '. . . the glow from the odd sixty watt bulb seemed hardly relevant'.

Though the blackout was so intrusive in the lives of the common man, it was not all doom and gloom for children. Ten-year-old Charles and his friends in Liverpool felt a wonderful sense of freedom as children of the blackout, playing in a twilight world where being unsupervised meant they did not have to curtail their wild adventures and self-made entertainment: 'So it was that as the days became shorter, our games became more adventurous as we devised new reasons for chasing each other up and down the stygian canyons which were our wartime playground once the sun had set . . . and at such speed, up and down the four foot wide back entries, on the backyard walls, in and out of the absolutely pitch black air-raid shelters, and getting free rides on the buffer bars of the slower moving trams.' Those blackout playgrounds provided Charles with great childhood memories of playing out; a childhood of scraped shins, bloody knees and endless, exhausting fun.

The blackout had a serious shortcoming, however. It may have made people safer from pinpoint enemy bombing but a new enemy took its place: the motor vehicle. Travelling by public transport in the blackout became a hazard due to partially-lit buses, trams and trains which were rendered almost invisible in the dark. There were no bright streetlights, no blazing shop windows and no signposts to show the way. Teenage Bill found travelling by bus in Dunstable at night proved difficult: '. . . knowing when to get off a bus at night was a real problem. All the windows were covered in stuck on anti-blast paper except for a postcard sized bit in the middle.' The buses crept along so slowly that Bill and his friends rode their bikes behind them, holding on 'with our front wheel six inches from the back and getting a lift'. Signalling a bus to stop and pick up passengers when neither the vehicle nor the people could be seen was problematic. Catching a bus involved furtively flashing a torch on and off, and the light had to be pointed at the ground to make sure it did not accidently signal a German bomber instead of the No. 28 bus.

Pitch-black railway stations, their signposts already removed, made train travel potentially dangerous as young Frank in West Sussex knew only too well: 'On the railways it was sometimes impossible to know at which station you had arrived because all the station place names had been removed or obliterated. Sometimes it was difficult to know whether the train had stopped or was still moving. Even if a train had stopped it may not have reached the station platform as often was the case . . . When this happened, the guard had to shout at the top of his voice warning passengers not to alight from the train!' In Liverpool, the blacked-out port made the docks a highly dangerous place. During the first nine months of the war, fifteen seamen drowned when they fell into the waters of the Mersey during blackout hours.[3]

Cars were very hard to spot on a dark night due to regulations stipulating that cardboard discs and layers of newspaper must cover front and rear car headlamps. Just to make sure cars could not be seen, in 1940 it became illegal to drive a light-coloured car.[4] It was not only motor vehicles that were difficult to see on a dark night, but pedestrians too. Grace made sure she always wore 'a button covered with luminous paint' pinned to her coat when she went out to help make her more visible to traffic. Policemen in Salford, who wore white uniforms for point duty, made themselves even more noticeable with a red electric bulb in their helmets.[5] Experiments with a 'star light' lighting system in London offered a glimmer of light in the first hour and the final hour of blackout time, but driving in dusk-like conditions made judging distances and speed far more difficult.[6] A 20mph speed limit in built-up areas became enforced on Britain's streets. This was tricky to adhere to during the blackout as dashboard lights were not allowed, making it difficult for drivers to tell just how fast they were going. The first vehicle to be caught exceeding the speed limit was a hearse.[7]

Despite the new speed limit, the overall rate of road accidents increased dramatically, especially during the blackout. The roads were lethal. An accident near Philip's house happened 'when a motorcyclist who failed to recognize a T-junction went straight into a wall on the opposite side'. Janet's father got a lift to London one evening and the driver, like 'a lot of people used to', drove on the white line in an attempt to see where he was going. Unfortunately, the car that was coming in the opposite direction appeared to be doing the same and they collided. The dramatic increase in the numbers of road accidents in just the first few months of the war saw the number of fatalities soar. Road casualties in Birmingham increased by 81 per cent and in Glasgow the figures trebled.[8] By the end of 1944, deaths on the road almost equalled the figure for those killed by bombing.[9] If the Germans didn't get you, the British motorist probably would.

Chapter 2

Air-Raid Shelters

. . . My father and the next-door neighbour dug a trench for us all to take shelter in. Shades of WW1.

Basil Stopps

In 1938 a father in Wanstead spent a few weeks in hospital after falling down an enormous gaping hole in his garden. Being an enterprising family man with four children, and fearing the worst might happen if he was ever called up, he had taken precautions to protect his family. The hole in the garden was his 'enormous DIY project', a task which took him nearly a year to complete. This was an underground air-raid shelter reinforced in 'a foot of concrete. All mixed by hand.' His seemingly crackpot project was the cause of much curtain twitching and raised more than a few eyebrows: 'Everybody thought he was mad at the time, including my mother.'

The Government spent much time deliberating the problem of protecting the public. Speculation abounded upon the likelihood of the intensity and effect of bombing and the number of casualties that would result. When the figures were based on the effects of aerial bombing by the Luftwaffe in the Spanish Civil War, the numbers of predicted fatalities were enormous. One solution for protecting British civilians was the field trench, tried and tested in the last war. Open dugouts and cut-and-cover trenches, lined and roofed, were dug in parks and open places by county councils across the country. While the councils were digging, industrious fathers prepared for war by enlisting their children to help dig their own family trenches at home. Six-year-old David in Stockport found himself spending a lot of time with a spade in hand, up to his knees in mud. He helped his father and brother excavate 'a trench five feet wide and eighteen feet long, through a shallow layer of earth and then into solid yellow clay down to a depth of about six feet'. Typically, being Britain, it began to rain 'and the trench quickly filled with water, and with the solid clay bed that water was there to stay'. Defeated by the British weather, the family had no choice but to fill in their waterlogged trench and stand by to watch as their neighbour, an engineer, designed and built 'a much grander project'. His monster of a trench was lined with brick walls, roofed with railway sleepers and capped with earth. This masterpiece attracted a lot of attention and was quite a talking-point in the neighbourhood.

Trenches were never going to be the solution to constant, long, nightly air raids, but they did have their uses. One boy's uncle, who had been wounded at Vimy Ridge in France during the last war, lived close to the bombing target of Kenley airfield. He utilised the defences he knew he would need – a slit trench with two budgies in a cage nearby as gas warning monitors. The trench saved his life when a Messerschmitt 110 machine-gunned the area in one last show of defiance before it plummeted to earth, wounding him and killing the budgies. However, trench shelters presented a problem. They were cold, wet and they were unpleasant to spend a great deal of time in, therefore many were never used. Basil's father's example was typical. In the late summer of 1939 he laboured with a neighbour in a field behind their homes in Essex. They dug a trench large enough to shelter both families from the forthcoming war, and then abandoned it: 'We never did use it or even mention it again, but such was the thinking at the time.' An alternative to the trench was to convert a room inside the house into a strong-room; and that was exactly what some people did.

An outside toilet was made into a shelter . . . I can't remember what we did when we needed the toilet.

Eleanor Tempest

On the day that war was declared, a father in Kent constructed an indoor fortress in his home. His son, R.J., spent his birthday excitedly watching as the dining room was converted. Scaffolding poles were sawn to length to support a board decking positioned just below the ceiling, the space between filled with sandbags and a small emergency supply of tinned food. The underneath of the solid oak dining table was designated as sleeping quarters. A large map of the world was stuck to one wall to complete the military HQ theme. Even when they had a new Anderson shelter delivered, they still preferred their home-built bunker and only the heavy bombing of the London Blitz could persuade them to go below ground.

David's father, unable to compete with the super-trench next door, set to work on bomb-proofing his house. The boards from the sodden trench were recycled and used to board up the lounge windows, hand-filled sandbags were built to create a 6ft-high blast wall, the lounge ceiling was reinforced with wooden posts and an extra ceiling beam added. When completed, a double bed for the grown-ups was placed in the lounge and raised on bricks, beneath which David and his brother slept. A schoolboy in south-east London helped his father bomb-proof their house by making 'screens across the windows, consisting of two layers of planks about four inches apart, filling the space in-between with sand'. This proved very effective when the house joining onto theirs house was later obliterated by a bomb and theirs remained standing.

Not everyone had the means or experience to fortify their rooms, so instead they turned to the safest place in their house. While one grandmother in Brighton hid in her broom cupboard, another grandmother in Derby sat puritanically in her coal cellar – a dark, cold room which made for a gloomy place to shelter. With the fortitude of conviction, she continued to endure the discomfort of the coal hole throughout the war, firmly believing that 'survival counted more than comfort'.

Cellars were a popular choice of shelter and help was available from the council to convert cellars into strong-rooms. Workmen from West Yorkshire Council constructed a cage from steel joists in the front cellar of Gordon's Victorian house to make a reinforced underground sleeping area.[1] In some streets, cellars were shared. The Liverpool

Corporation worked on ten-year-old Charles' cellar, joining his with the cellars of the houses on both sides and strengthening the whole lot with steel pit props and a corrugated roof. This reinforced communal cellar could hold 'nineteen of us crammed into a dungeon; a windowless, low roofed dungeon'. At first, Charles did not looking forward to spending even a minute down there, never mind being incarcerated for a whole night. Despite his misgivings he soon found that nights spent eating hot buttered toast cooked on a fork in front of an open fire in the cellar's hearth, along with 'lots of community singing and storytelling', was actually 'very congenial'. There was an element of risk sheltering in that cellar with an open fire considering they were 'within six feet of an operating gas main and visible pipes', but the general thinking in Charles' cellar was that it was better to 'be bombed in comfort'. The grandmother in Derby would not have approved.

Not every house had a suitable cellar, and being underground was not everyone's first choice of shelter; at least not until the serious bombing started. Some people put their faith in heavy furniture of which the kitchen table at the heart of the family home proved to be most popular. In the quiet Nottinghamshire village of Old Colwick one family chose a different option for heavy-furniture sheltering. They took to sleeping behind a large bookcase-cum-bureau, squeezed in with a terrified wirehaired fox-terrier that 'once disgraced himself' as 'he hated the guns booming'. In Royal Tunbridge Wells, teenage Yvonne spent many nights concertinaed against the living room wall in a recess with another substantial piece of furniture – the family's piano. The narrow confines of her chosen shelter meant she had to sleep in a yoga-type position, legs up the wall. If she had the choice she would have much rather stayed in bed regardless of the danger, a feeling echoed by one girl's great aunt who, on account of her age and inherent stubbornness, did remain in bed. The formidable aunt had great 'disdain for the enemy and preferred to carry on as if nothing was out of the ordinary', stoically sitting up poker-straight in bed 'knitting oiled socks or soft woollen vests for children in hospital'. She defended her decision by forthrightly declaring, 'I've lived through the last war and nobody is going to chase me from my home now.'

If household furniture did not offer sufficient protection, there was always the cupboard under the stairs. This was another popular option as it appeared to be general knowledge that the strongest structural points of a house were the staircase and the chimney. In his family home in Essex, young Basil's father, field trench forgotten, decided his family's first line of defence would be the under-stairs cupboard, but only with some modification. The staircase was strengthened with wooden beams, just to be on the safe side. Basil's dog, Mick, evidently agreed that this was indeed the best place to be and during the family's frequent rush to the shelter it was Mick who always seemed to be the first to scramble in. Their cupboard was well stocked with 'a first aid box containing bandages, dressings, burns and mustard gas ointments' and 'emergency food supplies, mainly tin foods and milk, tea and biscuits'. Mick's motivation may well have been more out of concern for his stomach than bombs.

Michael in Bath had no cellar so he sheltered, uncomfortably, in the cupboard under the stairs. The problem was one of size. His tiny cupboard was not designed to accommodate an entire family, and with two adults and three children crammed in, there was barely room to breathe. Despite this, the cupboard proved to be a life-saver. Bomb blasts from a direct hit on the houses behind Michael's in the 1942 bombing of Bath tore through his house, wrenching the door next to the stairs clean off its hinges while the terrified family huddled inside their tiny cupboard. The suction from the explosions bowed the bedroom walls and lifted and dropped the entire roof of their house; but Michael and his family, sardined under the stairs, remained unharmed.

For those who felt the need to take shelter, they made do with what they had, even if it meant holing up in the privy, of all places. One family in the Dingle area of South Liverpool decided not use their outdoor toilet as a shelter which was just as well because a bomb hit it. Six-year-old Eleanor and her family, who were also in Merseyside, did use their privy as an air-raid shelter. It presented as a ready-made brick surface shelter, the same size as an under-stairs cupboard but with the added benefit of somewhere to sit, for one at least. The privy was made homely with scatter cushions, a rug, a nice curtain at the door and a Tilly lamp. Fortunately, considering the heavy raids that would hit Merseyside, her family was later able to upgrade to a more substantial form of shelter: the garden Anderson.

'Mother called it bedlam'.
Noreen 'Betty' Powles

Portable steel shelters began to be distributed to the public in February 1939. The Anderson was a DIY garden shelter that consisted of corrugated steel sheets that were bolted together to form the roof and sides, with steel plate ends with a door hole cut into one. Each Anderson came with a set of instructions, a bag of nuts and washers, and a spanner. To be effective, the bottom half of the shelter had to be placed underground to help absorb blasts. The finished result resembled a partly-buried tin can.

Nine-year-old Brian in Southampton was one of the first in his area to get an Anderson because his father had a job as an Air Raid Inspector with the borough's engineering department. Households with an income less than £250 per year could claim a free Anderson. The uptake of Andersons appeared to be slow in Basil's area of Romford, Essex, as 'only one in four households had an Anderson shelter'. One reason why a family might not choose the Anderson option was that it was only feasible to have one if they had a garden big enough to build it in, and then they had to be prepared to dig a large, deep hole. This was not an easy task for anyone, especially mothers and children whose sons and fathers had gone to war. Help was available from local councils to erect shelters in such cases, but this involved making a claim for assistance. In the month before the war began, West Ham Council already had a waiting list of over 4,000 applications for help erecting Andersons.[2]

Preparing the ground and erecting the shelter was laborious. The digging necessary to make an underground pit was a gruelling task for those who had to dig through clay soil, or the chalk and flint bedrock of Croydon like Christine's family and neighbours in Waddon. They had to use pickaxes to dig giant holes to the regulation depth of a few feet. All the neighbours in Christine's street rallied around to help each other hew those back-breaking pits. Well before the war it was known that in areas where the water table was high, excavations for shelters would likely result in waterlogged holes. Those Andersons that could not be dug in, and so remained perched above ground, could be strengthened with a covering of rubble, earth and concrete. The cost and supply of materials was supposed to be met by local councils, but only if they could find a cheap supply of materials and if they were successful in getting a grant to meet the costs.[3] Sodden ground did not appear to be a problem in South Norwood where Colin's older brother and his war veteran father were successful in 'digging a big hole in the garden to make a dugout with parts of an old bedstead, just like he had done in France and Belgium'. Colin's father applied his knowledge of trench warfare to his enterprise, working on the principle of the deeper the better. With the hard work done they received delivery of their Croydon Corporation Anderson. Unfortunately, the scale of the colossal pit in their garden was somewhat larger than needed and when their eagerly-anticipated Anderson dropped into the hole it was completely lost. More digging ensued to refill the pit to the required size.

Excavations for air-raid shelters could spring some surprises. Teenage Joy and her father were industriously digging when they unearthed a body: '. . . after getting quite deep we found a piece of skeleton and then more was revealed. The skull, the spine and ribs!' This was not altogether surprising as their house had been built on top of an old church hall complete with a graveyard which had allegedly been emptied. Being dutiful citizens, they reported their find to the local police station but 'were somewhat horrified by the answer given by the very busy policeman on duty: "Oh Lewis, just chuck it over 't wall will yer, its busy 'ere."' In urban Mitcham, London, Irene had a friend who had a surprise when excavations for their Anderson also revealed bones. Eventually, the entire skeleton of a cow was dug out of the ground.[4]

Community spirit was strong in East Finchley where Henri lived. His father did his best to help their elderly neighbour who was partially deaf and could not hear the local air-raid siren. His idea was to use a large school hand-bell to alert her when there was an air raid. Unfortunately, his act of charity unwittingly caused terror in the street as the ringing of a bell – the signal for gas attack – sent neighbours fleeing in panic for their gas masks. Frank in Eastbourne had profoundly deaf parents. His neighbour came up with a practical plan of rigging up a 'bell push' on the outside wall of their semi, with the end of it located on the headboard of Frank's bed. In theory, when the neighbour rang the bell to sound the alert, the bell would wake Frank up. Privately, Frank thought there was 'something intrinsically barmy about the idea' for when he was sleeping lightly he could hear the air-raid siren sound the alert, but when he was deeply asleep not even the blasting of a siren, let alone a bell, could wake him.

Unfortunately, the sense of community engendered by neighbours pulling together could fall short on occasion. Yvonne's father did not have an Anderson shelter for his own family but he was asked by a lady neighbour if he would help her husband excavate a hole for their shelter. Yvonne's father 'gladly did but was not at all pleased to be told at the end of it that he was not welcomed there. The excuse, according to Her Ladyship, was that she didn't want a strange man in there with her and anyway men smelled more than women.' Not surprisingly, this did not go down well with Yvonne's father. The neighbour had no objection to females so Yvonne and her mother did use her shelter – but only when Yvonne's father was away working nights. Her Ladyship provided a light supper and, in those years of rationing, food could break down barriers; in fact, Yvonne would wait impatiently for the siren to wail because 'let's face it, it meant tea and biscuits'.

The finished Anderson shelter was a mere 6ft high and 4ft 6in wide and this small space was optimistically designed to sleep six. Teenager Rosemarie in London thought they were too small, and with her father being over 6ft tall and a big man there was barely any room to even sit in her Anderson. Sixteen-year-old East-Ender Ronald could not help but think it was a good thing his two brothers sheltered somewhere else because with his parents, their two lodgers, plus Jip the dog and Tibby the cat squeezed into the family Anderson, there really was literally not enough room to swing a cat. Andersons did come in an extra-large size. Christine had a large family of seven so they had 'an extra-long one', and in Gillingham, Kent, Jill's family had a 'double sized one' that was built beneath the garden fence to share with the neighbours. Whatever the size of the shelters, it appeared that some communities changed their minds about the necessity of Andersons when 1939 drew to a close with no sign of heavy bombing. In a disused railway siding at Scunthorpe, several railway wagons loaded with over 600 unwanted Andersons spent the winter in limbo. Scunthorpe households, who had applied for the shelters the year before, refused to take delivery of them. By the summer of 1940 with the Battle of Britain raging overhead, the residents of the town had a swift change of heart and warmly welcomed their Andersons.[5]

Shelters were notoriously prone to flooding and were always damp. The walls dripped with condensation and any bedding had to be taken out in the morning to be dried and aired. One boy in London found his Anderson was as cold as a fridge in winter and his clothes and bedding were perpetually soaked by water sliding down the corrugated metal surfaces. In addition to 'blankets, eiderdowns and hand-crocheted woollen quilts', his bunk was covered in old, heavyweight coats but 'pride still dictated that one didn't let neighbours know of one's plight or poverty by revealing that one was covered in bed by coats not quilts'. To his mother's complete mortification her children's bedtime routine revealed both 'when, after tucking her two kids in for the night in the shelter, the neighbours could hear the plaintive shouts of "Mum, Florrie's pulling the quilt off me and now she's been and gone and torn the sleeve off!"'

While the dark, damp environment of the Anderson shelter was not comfortable for people, it did not go completely unappreciated by other forms of life. One Anderson in Lewisham had a resident mouse. Thurza, her sister, and mother were found standing outside their shelter in the middle of a heavy night-time raid, too frightened to go back inside because of the unwelcome rodent lodger: 'Dad found us still there when he came off duty. "What are you doing out here you silly bleepers", he asked, "it's not safe, get back inside." . . . "If Hitler had dropped a load of mice instead of bombs, he'd have won this bleepy war."' In Bristol, ten-year-old David had an Anderson in his garden but it was unused for a while. Gradually it filled up with seeping rain until it was a foot deep in water. Being a perfect amphibian habitat it was requisitioned as a pond by the local frog population. Such was the dampness of garden Andersons that Robert's grandpa found his shelter proved to be an ideal location for fungiculture. His Anderson was 'cannily used for growing mushrooms – the dank environment being perfect for this malodorous task'.

However well decorated your shelter, nothing could compensate for that night-time awakening to move from bed to shelter, especially in the middle of winter. Never to be forgotten were the countless nights disturbed by the sounds of the siren wailing, the whine of bombs falling, ack-ack guns blasting, and the headlong, fear-filled hike down the garden. What Colin in Croydon really hated about winter night raids was 'getting out of a warm bed and running up the garden to the shelter, especially on frosty nights. And then, when the All Clear went, to get back into a cold bed. I hated Hitler.' Seven-year-old Betty in Derby was another child who hated being woken up for the dreaded shelter-run. She would plead to be allowed to 'die bombed in my own warm bed' but fortunately her parents 'ignored such requests and I would be bungled off to the shelter, shivering every inch of the way'. One boy's mother near Sawbridgeworth in Essex was most particular about the etiquette of the shelter-run. Her family's shelter was situated a hundred yards down the garden but it was not speed that counted, it was 'the G.A. Henty ideal of steadfastness under fire' that took precedence. When a sudden raid took the household by surprise, Emily the cook 'very sensibly sprinted, ahead of us all, towards the air-raid shelter', but Mother 'regarded this swift response as cowardice in the face of the enemy and as the setting of a thoroughly bad example to the young'. The cook was made to stop and stand 'until the children, all six of us, had walked past her in a calm crocodile to the shelter'.

Maurice's family were allocated carrying duties for their rush to the shelter. Maurice carried the pillows, his brothers took the blankets, and his mother lugged an old box stuffed full of important family documents such as ration books and birth certificates. Ernest's mother in Leeds carried meat – the family's ration joint: it was the only way they could get the dog into the shelter. Jill was usually running with her dinner. The raids that happened during mealtimes were a real nuisance, especially when children had to wait for a lull in the raid so that their mother could dash back to the kitchen to make the pudding. 'We often ate by instalments.' Little Eleanor's family had their shelter kit pre-packed by the back door for a quick getaway. This included a cushion each for head protection, one hand holding the cushion and the other hand holding onto the person in front as they walked in crocodile formation to the neighbour's Anderson. Jean's mother made sure she had got coffee. Her routine when they got into their shelter on an evening was to put the coffee percolator on the little paraffin stove. It took over three hours to make; but then, they did have all night.

While some little children clutched their teddies on their trip to the shelter, others took something to help while away the hours. Entertaining and distracting children in the confines of a shelter could be difficult. Nine-year-old June played I Spy in her shelter, though it was not a game that lasted long. She also wrote poetry. Betty and her siblings took their 'Rupert Bear books to the shelter, and playing cards, reading by torchlight. It was easy to cheat at the card games and many a small war developed in the shelter because of this.' With two children and a baby to keep occupied, it was not surprising that 'Mother called it bedlam'.

One way to keep warm during the shelter-run was to wear a siren suit. Siren suits were the onesies of wartime. Even the Prime Minister Winston Churchill wore his bespoke siren suits of green velvet and pinstripe in public. Betty privately thought it made him look like 'a chubby elf'. Soon many children were wearing a siren suit as an air-raid fashion favourite. Janet's outfit for the shelter-run was a siren suit worn South Yorkshire style – paired with wellingtons and a blanket slung around the shoulders – while little Maureen in

Staffordshire wore a soft china-blue number that she was particularly fond of: 'It was cosy and warm and woolly and I felt very special in it, being carried into the garden in the night.' One twelve-year-old girl in Barnsley was struggling to maintain her shelter-run panache as she was not too happy with the coarseness of her siren suit, no doubt because her mother had made it 'out of an old stiff blanket'. Mary Lou had a 'rust-coloured and scratchy' siren suit but she did not mind, it was bona fide air-raid apparel and as such she felt ever so 'proud in it'.

Despite the Anderson's shortcomings, it did offer physical and psychological protection: '. . . but for all the discomfort and lack of sleep, we did feel less vulnerable when we heard the drone of German planes . . . and heard the bombs exploding'. Colin's neighbours who refused to have a shelter as they 'were not going to live like rats', soon changed their minds when the raids started, at which point Colin wryly observed 'they were the first into ours'. When Jill attended St Mary's Convent School in Romford, she wrote a school essay at the age of seven on 'The Story of a Piece of Coal'. She described herself as a piece of coal 'in a coal-bunker with my parents, and how anxious I was about being taken from the cosy bunker, and what a relief it was when the other pieces of coal came and covered us up safely – a selfish but a natural instinct – it was the other pieces of coal, not me and my family, who were in danger'. When she reread her schoolgirl essay in later life, she realized that 'the subconscious fear I was expressing [was] about air raids, about the threat of separation and death'. However deep down underground you were, your fears remained on the surface.

They were totally uninhabitable by being used as toilets.
Terry Middleton

Irene in Mitcham had a different type of shelter in her garden – a domestic surface shelter. Hers was 'square, built of brick and stood above ground. It had a flat concrete roof and was quite near the house.' She did not like it very much as it looked like it could easily fall down, 'the cement between the bricks looked very sandy'. She sat in there on the wooden bunks during night raids with her mother and brother, an umbrella held over their heads because the roof leaked like a sieve.[6] A six-year-old girl in South London also had a garden brick-built shelter, 'a small one about as roomy as a small garden shed, with three very narrow bunks'. Like the Anderson there was not a lot of room so her father, a big man, found it hard to fit in the shelter, never mind squeezing onto one of the bunks. One father in Kent went the extra mile by constructing his own brick-built shelter as an extension to his shared Anderson. He plastered the walls, added ventilation pipes and furnished it with 'double bunk beds three feet wide, a table with a sink under, a sliding panel in the top and a drawer for baby to sleep in'.

Surface shelters appeared on many streets to be used as places of safety for public use, particularly after the manufacture of Andersons ground to a halt in early 1940 when steel was diverted to the war effort. These surface shelters were useful should anyone be caught outdoors during a raid or if they did not have a suitable shelter at home. Some were blast- and splinter-proof, but none of them were bomb-proof. They were built in brick, above ground, on a concrete base with a concrete roof like Irene's shelter, and were rectangular in shape. The other thing they had in common with Irene's shelter was that many of them were not safe. Some of these surface shelters were constructed with mortar made without cement during 1940 when cement supplies for shelter-building were limited.[7] As a result, hundreds of communal surface shelters were prone to teetering dangerously whenever a bomb landed nearby. With collapsing walls and falling roofs, these street shelters became known as the 'Morrison sandwich' after the Home Secretary Herbert Morrison.[8] By March 1941 the Government had little choice but to demolish these economically-built shelters at considerable cost, pulling down 560 brick surface shelters in Harrow alone, though this still left many badly-constructed shelters built without proper reinforcement on the streets. Coventry suffered from collapsing brick shelters, and in Bristol 21,000 people found themselves without shelters when their faulty surface shelters either fell down or were pulled down.[9] In West Bromwich the council demolished 170 public shelters that had been made with lime mortar, including those in the cathedral graveyard which were so badly built that children were known to be able to dislodge the bricks with a push of the hand.[10]

Communal public shelters sprang up everywhere but spending a night with strangers was not a popular choice. Irene, with her not-fit-for-purpose garden shelter, occasionally resorted to using the public shelter in Dahlia Gardens. This one had metal bunk beds placed in rows inside.[11] One little boy who was also in London used the 'a big public shelter in nearby Acton Playing Fields' at the beginning of the war, but it was 'noisy and crowded, and Mother didn't like having to sit next to all those "common people."' She was not the only person who did not like public shelters. Seven-year-old Peter and his mother sometimes had to use a public shelter if the siren sounded whilst they were out shopping in South London. Peter loathed these and later attributed his claustrophobia as originating from his forced confinement in surface shelters. The quality of a person's communal shelter experience depended on which shelter was used. Location and clientele were important factors. Yvonne's father, being unwelcome in Her Ladyship's Anderson-dining-shelter, insisted that when he was home his family must use 'the public shelter down the hill'. Yvonne took a great dislike to this particular public shelter, partly because it was icy cold and perpetually damp, but mostly because of its 'inhospitable atmosphere with all the locals sitting on deck chairs, silent and morose'. The main public shelter in the town was, in Yvonne's opinion, much better as at least it was 'full of folks who were jolly and chattered. Class distinction was levelled and the ladies of higher breeding at least put on a good show of mingling with us lower orders, dunking their biscuits with cheerful abandon.' When her father happily nodded off to sleep in the dank shelter down the hill, Yvonne and her mother would surreptitiously tip-toe out in silent protest and sneak back home, though her father 'wasn't very happy of course when he awoke and found himself sitting there like a lemon'.

The aversion to public shelters led many to be semi-abandoned. In North London, Terry found that his area was dominated by squalid shelters which people were using as public urinals. Adrian who lived in Warwick Crescent had noticed the same, and that in addition 'vagrants took to living in them'. This was not just confined to London. In the town of Taunton in Somerset, there were many street shelters that were unused. These were avoided not only for their neglected interiors but because of fears that they were dangerous as they were 'constructed on a concrete raft poured directly on a road surface, with no foundations'. Schoolboy Harding gave these shelters a wide berth as it was known that 'where one of these had sustained a near miss there were stories of the whole thing being slid along the road several feet by the blast'. The heavy concrete roofs were also known to be dangerous. Adrian witnessed the consequences of this when a bomb landed in a residential area not far from his home. The blast caused the roofs of nearby street shelters to collapse, killing the families inside: 'I remember an ARP warden telling father that if the people had stayed indoors under the stairs most of them would have survived.' There was always an exception to the rule as eleven-year-old Londoner Richard discovered when a 'blockbuster bomb' flattened a wide area of shops and homes nearby. The only building he could see that was still left standing was a solitary brick-built shelter.

Super-sized brick shelters were built to house large groups of people. In Kinning Park, Glasgow, 'a long brick building big enough to hold fifty to sixty people' was erected to shelter the occupants of the densely-packed tenements of Marlow Street where ten-year-old William lived. William felt that the community were happy sharing the shelter as 'we were glad of the company as we huddled together during the many air raids'. There was, unfortunately, a major problem which appeared to have been overlooked by the council's planning department: 'As there was no other place to put our shelter it was built up against the railway wall on a piece of spare ground around the corner where nearby stood a Bonded Warehouse some thirty yards across the way. The railway was a main supply line and the "Bondie" housed large quantities of volatile scotch whisky, and it didn't take a genius to realize we were sitting between two prime targets for the Jerry planes.'

AIR-RAID SHELTERS

In the tenements of Glasgow there was not always enough room to build shelters and so a substitute was offered: the strutted close mouth version. Tenement closes were reinforced with timber and braced, which provided a pocket of protection against the collapse of the buildings. These shelters proved unpopular as the open entrance was often exposed to the bitter cold, wind and rain. They were however an improvement on many of Glasgow's surface shelters which were renowned for lack of doors, seats, lavatories and even roofs.[12] Abandoned shelters were often targets of vandalism. By the winter of 1942, Glasgow faced a bill of over £50,000 to repair the city's damaged shelters; schoolchildren and teenagers were largely held to blame for the wanton destruction.[13]

So now we were admonished to get into this cage for the night.
I felt a right Charlie squatting in there with two others.
G. 'Yvonne' Dalton

The 1941 indoor alternative shelter was the Morrison. It cost on average £7 12s 6d. Families on a household income of below £350 per year could have a Morrison for free. The Morrison came in kit form of 359 parts to assemble with three tools, and the completed project produced a large table, 6ft 6in long and 2ft 5in high, with a solid steel top, removable wire-mesh sides and a sprung mattress floor. Two-tier bunk bed versions were also available. It was cumbersome, restrictive and cage-like, but it did offer protection if the house collapsed. The problem was that this shelter was big. For the working-class people who needed a Morrison the most – those living in the small terraces and tenements of major industrial areas where heavy bombing was likely – there was simply no room in their houses for a shelter of this size.

Putting the Morrison together was a major DIY job, but luckily there were Boy Scouts like Tottenhall Terry. Armed with a spanner, he helped assemble Morrison shelters in homes in London, though he was 'not sure how well our efforts held together – I just hope none of them was tested for real!' Michael received one but personally he did not quite trust this new-fangled shelter, conceding that it probably was 'a little more secure than our cupboard under the stairs', but somehow 'it didn't feel so safe'. Tired of their domestic surface shelter and the public shelter, Irene's family opted for a Morrison. It took several men to manhandle it into the house and bolt it all together.[14] In David's house in Stockport, having experienced trench building and home-based bunker DIY, they eagerly awaited arrival of their Morrison. This big, solid iron piece of furniture 'took up a double mattress in width and covered just over half its length' and for David must have been an improvement on sleeping beneath his parent's bed. The Morrison's awkward size was unfortunately responsible for the deep gash in his head when he misjudged his flying leap into it one night and had to be stitched up in Stockport Infirmary. With its sharp metal corners, it was best to be careful negotiating your way past the Morrison, but it was worth it. Dorothy viewed her aunt's new Morrison as her saviour as it meant she was at last cosy, warm and happy rather than spending nights in the cat-smelling, flea-ridden Anderson. For teenager Audrey and her family, the newly-installed Morrison meant that when the devastating landmines fell on the city of Sheffield they at least had some protection, cramped though they were with 'two adults, two children, a dog and a number of toys' as well as 'essential emergency rations of food and water', all squeezed in together inside a metal cage.

The Morrison, despite its unwieldy weight and size, could be a useful multi-purpose piece of furniture. One boy in London had his Morrison in the dining room and it made for 'an excellent table tennis table', and Audrey's Morrison, which was kept in their large kitchen, added an authentic touch to playtime: 'I used to pretend I was an animal in a zoo, because we were really in a cage.' A teacher in Essex used her Morrison at home as a school table for when she was teaching children whose school had closed. Jill was one of those pupils sitting around the Morrison in this teacher's house, ready to dive into the cage if the air-raid siren sounded. Frank was not impressed with the Morrison. He got his at the time of the 1944 V1 bombing attacks: 'We tried it a couple of times, but it was most uncomfortable, so it remained a great obstruction in the living room, covered with a cloth and with vases on it, until the V1 threat disappeared, and so, mercifully, did the shelter.' For teenage Yvonne who preferred a bed, but not this bed, the Morrison was just another form of embarrassment. It just did not feel right crouching in a steel cage with your parents. At least she could stay at home and did not have to face the trial of sheltering with the many thousands who crowded into the jam-packed depths of the London Underground.

> *People slept on the platform, sometimes perilously close to the edge; there was no privacy and the toilet facilities usually meant a bucket behind a curtain.*
>
> *Adrian Cooper*

There was no doubt that Tube stations were the people's choice of shelter in London. Because they were so deep underground they were considered relatively safe and they had been used as shelters in the Great War. They also had an advantage over other types of shelter: you could not hear the bombing. The Government was not in favour of mass sheltering because of the potential for high numbers of fatalities should a large shelter be hit, nor was it keen on deep-level shelters which might encourage an underground mentality where people might live permanently down in the Tube while the city burned above. In addition, the Government wanted to keep the Underground solely as a transport system for the war effort. When the Blitz began the police barricaded the entrance to Liverpool Street Station and faced a stand-off with determined Londoners seeking shelter. With Bobbies in front of them and bombs at their backs, the public were not going to be thwarted for long. Within twenty days of the start of the London Blitz, 177,000 people were settling down in the Tube on a nightly basis.[15]

Tube trekkers were highly visible in London. Richard saw many of the families where he lived in London heading towards the Tube stations just before teatime each day, bags packed and children in tow. This was not unusual; it was 'common practice'. Rosemarie saw them as she cycled to school each morning through West Acton where lots of 'people carrying rugs and other paraphernalia' were making the morning vigil home or to work from the Tube stations. These Tube-trekking families provided a surprising source of income for one local man. He may have been 'considered unemployable before the war' but he had the common sense to spot a unique business opportunity. He started a personal Tube courier service: 'From somewhere, he acquired an old basinet pram. With this he would obtain contracts to carry sheets, mattresses and the like to the Underground station for a small fee.'

Concerns about the living conditions in the Tube stations were the reason Adrian and his mother refused to use them: 'People slept on the platform, sometimes perilously close to the edge; there was no privacy and the toilet facilities usually meant a bucket behind a curtain. Stepping off a late night train meant picking your way over sleepers to the escalators and that alone put mother off joining them.' Many children slept in the Tube and this occurred throughout the war, not just during the height of the Blitz. On the night of 19 January 1942, with the temperature plummeting to freezing and 6in of snow on the ground, nearly 600 children spent the night in Tube shelters.[16]

On occasion, Ronald used Old Street Station when he had to escape from the two horrors in his life – the heavy bombing and his cramped Anderson shelter. It was very boring for a teenage boy to be in the station for hours on end and so he would pass the time by joyriding the trains from station to station for fun. Back at Old Street Station after riding the trains, Ronald would frequently find that his space had disappeared in a sea of bodies. Invariably, the only sleeping spaces left were for latecomers who had to exchange the danger of bombing for the danger of sleeping precariously on the edge of the platform. Ronald's morning wake-up call was usually 'the unwelcome noisy and draughty arrival of the first train about twelve inches from my head'.

In response to the Blitz, the Government reconsidered the need for deep shelters and planned to excavate new deep-level shelters linked to existing stations. One tunnel was abandoned as it posed a threat to the foundations of St Paul's Cathedral and another became waterlogged, but eight were finally completed by March 1942. These

100ft-deep tunnels had separate fortified entrances and each shelter could accommodate up to 8,000 people, but they remained closed to the public until the menace of the V1 flying bombs forced the opening of five of them to the public in July 1944.[17] Tickets were issued to regular Tube trekkers and the homeless, but these deep-level tunnels were not popular. Dorothy used one and it was without doubt her 'nightmare'. Her family had an entrance card allowing them into the Raleigh section of a deep shelter and it listed their allocated tunnel section and bunk numbers. The sleeping arrangements in Dorothy's tunnel were far removed from her bedroom at home: 'Rows and rows of metal framed bunks lined these claustrophobic warrens. I occupied a top one alongside a curved concrete wall. To be enclosed with hundreds of sweating, sighing bodies after the silence of my own bedroom was alarming, and the man directly opposite on the top bunk was a real snorer.' The lack of privacy bothered Dorothy as, 'too embarrassed to strip in front of strangers, I wore most of my nightwear under day clothes. To get ready for bed I would shut my eyes and hoped that no one was looking as I undressed under the blankets.' Despite this there was a sense of community: 'Some sections appeared jolly with accordion players and singers . . . Whenever I could I escaped to wander through other tunnels which seemed friendlier than where I was. We made temporary friends and looked out for them each evening. If any missed a night we wondered if they were still alive.' Dorothy did her best to make the best of a bad situation, but the stress of Underground sheltering and all the bombing she had experienced caused her skin to 'break out in itching sores' and she suffered from 'disturbed dreams'. Even when she started work in 1944 she could never bear to travel by Tube 'just in case I got blocked in'.

Dorothy's worries of being trapped deep underground were not unfounded. Nothing was safe from a direct hit. A total of 200 people lost their lives in the bombing of Bounds Green, Marble Arch and Balham stations, and many fatalities occurred at other stations. The bomb that hit Bank station took the lives of fifty-six people, thirteen of who were teenagers. One Tube station did have its entrance blocked, as the girls feared, but not by a bomb. The crowd that was entering

Bethnal Green station on 3 March 1943, panicked and 178 people, including children and babies, died in the crush. Yet still the Underground continued to be used because people had a better chance below ground in a warren of tunnels when the city was being pounded by heavy bombing. Even when the war had ended there were around 12,000 homeless people still living in Tube stations until they were finaly evicted.[18]

For those in the city who avoided the Tube but still needed communal public shelters, there were many alternatives, including warehouses. In an ice storage warehouse sat thirteen-year-old Pamela. Pamela's mother had to take her children to the warehouse as it was her nearest available shelter, but they did not like it at all: 'It was very noisy, very hot, no privacy whatsoever and not very clean.' Every afternoon the family carried all their bedding to the warehouse and brought it all back home again the following morning – for months on end. The last straw was the day Pamela's mother discovered her children were riddled with head lice and infected with scabies. Tilbury shelter in Stepney was an enormous warehouse that gained a reputation for its appalling living conditions and was often overcrowded. The queues for night-time sheltering at Tilbury would form well before the shelter was open for the night. When the MP for West Fife visited Tilbury during a day-time air raid, he was puzzled to find long queues resolutely standing firm outside both ends of the tunnel despite anti-aircraft guns booming and the imminent threat of bombing. Tilbury was open but it appeared that people refused to go in before the night opening time of 5.30pm. If they did, then they would be booted out when the All Clear was signalled, which meant queuing all over again to get in for the night.[19] This notorious shelter was often visited by the police in the early hours to sort out fracas from fistfights in the men's WC, thieving and abusive behaviour to the wardens. Despite a strict policy on barring the entrance of unaccompanied children below the age of fourteen, lone children would evade the wardens and run loose in the shelter bays. For protection against infection and disease in communal shelters the wearing of hygienic face masks and use of antiseptic sprays was recommended,[20] and Tilbury made full use of the latter. In the summer of 1944 an over-zealous hygiene regime began in an attempt to tackle the smell and sanitation problem caused by flooded urinals, filth and unclean bedding. Cleaners resorted to using an over-concentrated solution of disinfectant using one gallon of carbolic per day rather than the recommended five gallons per month. Within the first few days of Tilbury's deep clean, sickness was reported and a fifteen-year-old girl was rushed to hospital suffering a severe asthma attack.

Even before the Government began digging deep shelters below London's Underground, many district and borough councils had prepared for war by tunnelling deep into the bedrock of Britain. In Ramsgate an underground metropolis grew in the newly-created deep subway, the 'Wind Tunnels', that were built to shelter up to 60,000 people. Pre-existing caves provided a natural choice of shelter. Below the city of Nottingham lay a honeycomb of ancient sandstone caves that dated from the Dark Ages. The Nottingham caves, which had at one time been medieval pauper holes that sheltered the unfortunate, were now sheltering those in need once again. One previously-inhabited natural cave was St Clements in Hastings. This small cave had a notorious history for being a den of iniquity, but it was opened in 1940 as an air-raid shelter capable of holding 500 people before being turned into a dance hall at the end of the war. One of the biggest cave systems was Chislehurst in Kent. These were old chalk and flint mines which became a well-known refuge for the bombed-out and homeless. They evolved into a thriving subterranean town and there was a high demand for places with long waiting-lists of people who had been displaced through war and misfortune.

Joan's mother in Deptford had tried the Anderson, the public shelters and the Underground, but she did not particularly like any of them. When she heard about the Chislehurst caves she took her daughter and baby by train to the caves where around 15,000 people were sheltering. It was a scary experience to enter the cave for the first time with only the tiny flame of a candle to cut through the darkness. At first, Joan and her mother 'went home during the day, but then it got too much for Mum and we stayed there all the time'. Conditions got better when electric light and bunk beds were installed, and soon a whole community developed at Chislehurst: 'They built a hospital in the caves and a concert place. We had nurses and doctors in case of illness or accidents, and anyone who could sing or dance or do anything at all could entertain us – so we didn't do too bad.' They were at least together, unlike many other families which found themselves divided by war and evacuation.

Chapter 3

Evacuation

We were all wildly excited and thought we were going on holiday and I couldn't understand why my mother looked so glum.

Jo Veale

Early in the morning of 3 September 1939, a 'rotund, amiable' taxi driver nicknamed 'Barrage Balloon' set off from Golders Green Station taxi-rank to a Hampstead Garden suburb in London. There he collected fifteen-year-old Audrey, her two sisters, a cocker spaniel and a portable wireless, all of whom were to be evacuated to distant family in Bedford. They drove all the way to Bedford with the hood down as all three girls were carsick. In Acton, five-year-old Brian found himself at first light on Sunday morning sitting with trepidation in the back of his father's BSA car as they tried to beat the exodus out of London. They drove out of the City really early before all the main roads were closed at 6.00am to 'allow for coaches transporting evacuees out of the capital'. He was going to live with his uncle for the next two years. Terry was one of nine squeezed uncomfortably into a Morris Cowley family saloon car that chugged out of London on the beginning of a long drive to Wales. Just waking up from an uncomfortable night on the floor at Warwick Senior School was six-year-old Robert. With his headmaster father striding in the lead, Robert's family set off at dawn to Victoria Station to join all the other refugees from Pimlico, London. Evacuation had begun.

The National Evacuation Scheme, code-named Operation Pied Piper, was entirely voluntary but there was pressure to 'do the right thing' as advertised in information leaflets and on billboard posters. Despite this, the figures fell unexpectedly short of the predicted 3.5 million as less than half that number took part. Many people opted for private evacuation, preferring to keep their children within the family, however distant. Others simply decided to stay at home and take their chances, and that decision was on occasion taken by the children themselves. Seven-year-old Donald in Bristol made his feelings clear: 'I refused point blank to go.' Essex boy Basil and his sister also adamantly refused to evacuate – there was no way they were leaving their mother on her own at night as their father worked night shifts. One mother in London decided her son Bill, aged eleven, was not going because if they 'were going to die in the bombing we would all go together'. An eight-year-old in Kent had a family with the same viewpoint: '. . . stay together – and perish together if that was what fate had in store'.

While parents in the hot-spots of cities such as London, Birmingham and Sheffield agonized over parting with their children, some children thought it was all very exciting. Eleven-year-old Eric in Newcastle could not quite grasp the significance of the situation as it felt like it was all 'a big adventure'. Jo from Birmingham, aged six, was 'wildly excited' as she was utterly convinced she was going on holiday and could not understand why her mother was so unhappy about it. East London girl Phyl, also six, also thought she was going on holiday, at least that was what her parents had told her, 'just for a few weeks', and her father promised to come and get her 'as soon as the silly war was over' and 'definitely in time for Christmas'. She did return home for Christmas, but not until Christmas 1945.

Other children were just as distraught as their parents. At Christine's house, five children and their mother huddled around the wireless on the Saturday night, waiting for the evacuation of Croydon to be announced. In twenty-four hours they were going and they did not know where. Everyone cried.

Richard's father in London sat down with his nine-year-old son for an important talk: he had to be evacuated for his 'own good . . . because war was coming'. Richard's mother wept quietly and nine-year-old Richard took it with grim stoicism: 'It was not really a talk because I just accepted it with a stiff upper lip, very British.' Edna in Hull did not even know that her mother had evacuation in mind. Being a fourteen-year-old school leaver, she made herself useful by helping the teachers with the evacuation day preparation. She made such each pupil had their carrier bag of rations – 'a tin of corned beef, biscuits, a few sweets, and a change of clothing' – and she responsibly escorted the little ones onto the waiting bus. As she turned to step off the bus her mother stopped her and said, '"Get back on." I said, "Why?" and she replied, "Because you are being evacuated." I said, "I'm not," and she said, "You are."' And so Edna found herself on the bus to Selby, leaving behind her mother and all eleven of her siblings to be an evacuee for an unhappy few months until her mother finally let her return home.

While the early birds were driving out of London, many children were on foot. Processions of gas mask-toting, bag-carrying, labelled children made their way to their designated departure points to board trains or buses. Richard kept his stiff upper lip – 'it may have quivered a little though' – as he marched like a soldier to the Underground, his embarkation point, with his tearful mother. Little Phyl made her way to Waterloo Station with her mother, her twelve-year-old sister and brother aged ten, each carrying their suitcases and gas-mask boxes. They boarded a train at Waterloo and it was only at this point that Phyl realized that their mother was not coming with them. Suddenly this supposed holiday just did not seem like a holiday after all. Bundled into the guards van of the train, the children caught 'a final glimpse of mum waving goodbye'. Distraught Phyl and her siblings were very close to tears as they travelled to Axminster where they began 'a life totally alien to anything we had ever known'.

Children coped with the upheaval and separation each in their own way. Six-year-old Ronald in Birmingham clutched his paper bag of jam sandwiches as he was separated from his brothers and sister. He travelled to the railway station in a coachload of little children who had all said goodbye to their parents; there were lots of tears but the bolder boys covered their fears 'with a little boy's bravado'. Richard's coping mechanism was to shut down, internalising the turmoil of being separated from home, his parents and all he had ever known. A lot of the other children seemed to have brothers and sisters with them, but being an only child he was on his own. By the time he was on the Tube, which he found frightening, inside a carriage 'filled with wailing', he had 'written himself off' and obviously found it all too harrowing: 'I felt dead, all my previous life had left me. I had no way to handle what was happening, so I withdrew into myself . . . I had always believed that Mum and Dad ran my world and protected me. Now all was chaos.'

Not every child felt upset or afraid. For some, it was completely the opposite. Eric was one of thousands of schoolchildren at Walkergate Railway Station, Newcastle upon Tyne. As he climbed aboard a steam train he felt as if he was beginning 'the adventure of a lifetime'. Eleven-year-old Muriel from Essex had arrived by bus at Tilbury Docks with other children from East Thurrock Primary School. They were about to embark on a Thames paddle steamer, the *Crested Eagle*. Muriel was elated to be on board, setting off to the unknown in the style of a true adventurer as she sailed with high hopes to the port of Felixstowe in Suffolk.

As buses rolled out of the cities and trains steamed through the countryside, processing centres along their routes were preparing for the influx. In Colchester, St John's Green School was one of several Colchester schools appointed as evacuee processing centres for East End Londoners on their way to the Essex countryside. Local schoolchildren were enlisted to help, including a class from Hamilton Road Senior School where thirteen-year-old John was a pupil. Their job was to issue the evacuees with bags of 'iron rations' which included 'a tin of corned beef, tin of milk, packet of biscuits, quarter pound of Cadbury's milk chocolate, as well as other things'. John had the important job of chocolate monitor. The pupils passed 'brown paper carrier bags along the tables, each boy putting in our particular contribution, it was just like a factory production line'. After a few days the last evacuees had gone and John, having done his bit in the National Evacuation Scheme, felt a sense of 'patriotic pride'. He was also pleased at his own personal achievement – at no point did he eat any of the chocolate.

Many of those first evacuees of 1939 returned home during the quiet period known as the 'Phoney War' when the expected heavy bombing did not happen. In 1940 it all changed when the waves of war reached the shores of Britain. A subsequent evacuation took place: the clearing of children from the stretch of coastline between Sussex and Norfolk which was a potential invasion point, plus the re-evacuation once again of children from cities designated as prime targets. Pat was one of many children evacuated from the East Coast to the West of England in 1940 after the Fall of France. She heard about it 'on the BBC News at nine o'clock on Sunday 2nd June 1940' and had only one week to prepare. It was 'very distressing' for her family and was the only time she was ever to see her father cry.

Fifteen-year-old Joyce was one of hundreds of evacuees being relocated from Kent coastal schools, all assembled on Folkestone railway station to begin their early morning journey, 'each carrying trunk, gas mask, lunch pack, tennis racquet, etc'. Brighton was another town evacuated. Christine had not long arrived there, having had to move from her first destination in her 1939 evacuation in order to join her evacuated school. The two Croydon schools, Lady Edridge and Christine's school which had been sharing premises with Brighton's Whitehawk School, were all getting ready to relocate once again due to the threat of invasion. Christine headed off to Woking while the rest of her family who had remained in their first billet were given just twenty-four hours in which to pack and leave because of its coastal location. They returned to Croydon and then, due to bombing, had to move yet again – twice more in fact until they ended up in the comparative safety of York, until that too got bombed. Finally, the whole family gave up trying to keep ahead of the bombing and reunited back in London.

In Glasgow it was the summer of 1940 when Sheena's family discovered that living in the shadow of a major Luftwaffe target, one of Scotland's largest armament factories, was not the best place to be. A family decision was made 'amid heartbreak' that the two daughters,

Sheena aged thirteen and Norma aged eight, should go to their aunt in Canada for an indefinite amount of time known as the 'Duration'. In a school in Liverpool, Kitty and her sister from Blackburn, Lancashire, stood in a line of children queuing for medicals and head lice inspection. Both Sheena and Kitty, with their sisters, were to travel under a scheme called the Children's Overseas Reception Board (CORB) which was a radical attempt by the British Government to protect the children of Britain by evacuating them overseas in what was to be a provisional exile. Some British 'sea-vacs' were sent abroad privately with their parents covering the cost, while over 26,000 children between the ages of five to fifteen were optimistically approved under the government funded CORB scheme to relocate to Canada, South Africa, Australia and New Zealand. Children were separated into two categories for administration purposes: state elementary and secondary schools, and non-grant-aided schools. As 'ambassadors' of Britain, the children selected for overseas evacuation should, it was agreed by the Government, be the best that Britain could offer and not the 'difficult' or unwanted. The 'best' had to be those who passed a medical examination and were preferably not under the care of the Poor Law or from orphanages.[1] The CORB scheme exported around 3,000 children before it ended in catastrophe in September 1940. A ship full of child evacuees sailing to Canada was torpedoed on its journey, resulting in the death of seventy-seven children.

People left London during the great Blitz in 1940 which saw around 40,000 schoolchildren evacuated out of the city. Many evacuated on their own initiative like Bill's family from Brentwood who decided enough was enough and evacuated themselves to their Welsh relatives in Dowlais Top. It was a shock for Jill to suddenly find her family evacuating from Chadwell Heath to Hertfordshire with no warning: 'I got up as usual and suddenly found we were going out, with suitcases.' She did not even have time to pack her books and toys, or say goodbye to friends and neighbours. Her father was moving the family as 'he had enough of sleepless nights', but as far as his daughter was concerned it was tantamount to 'running away, as I saw it'. Leaving their helpless neighbour, who had recently had a stroke, made Jill 'feel guilty and I felt my parents were wrong, but I couldn't argue with them. I had to do as I was told.' She felt terrible about her abrupt departure and desertion of her neighbour and as a consequence 'it haunted me for years'.

In 1941 Bristol was blitzed and David was one of the casualties of bombing in this city which had once been considered a safe area. He was offered evacuation to Cornwall and even though he did not have any idea where Cornwall was, he jumped at the chance to get away. If he stayed in Bristol he could easily have suffered the same fate as his father who had very recently been killed in the bombing. Dressed 'like a lumber-jack in miniature' in clothes from the Canadian Red Cross, having lost his own clothes when he was bombed out, twelve-year-old David found himself at Lawrence Hill Station ready to experience his first ever long train journey. His mother and two sisters remained in Bristol and David would not see them for many months until they visited, looking pale and gaunt after narrowly surviving being bombed out yet again. Maurice was also evacuated from Bristol with his 'pillow case with few belongings . . . and a bag with cucumber sandwiches' as he boarded a double-decker bus. To him it was 'one big adventure' with a train full of eager children. He was not yet to know that terrible homesickness would soon cause him to return home. Bombing, it seemed, was easier to cope with than the desperate longing to be home.

The use of German rockets and missiles in 1944 and 1945 forced further departures from London and the South. As an evacuee veteran of the first wave, Alan felt more confident about his second evacuation in 1944 than his first in 1939, and this time he was not upset. He had been traumatized by a near miss from a doodlebug and felt 'fed up with sleeping down the shelter every night'. He would rather be well out of the way. Compared to staying at home with Hitler's rockets, evacuation seemed positively welcoming.

I'LL TAKE THAT ONE. Yes, that happened to me.
Alan Hall

Evacuees Clive and his mother arrived in the village of Shackerstone,

Leicestershire. They lasted three days. 'It was too quiet!' declared Clive's mother as she fled back home to Birmingham. At Pagham cricket club, picking up their rations, were new arrivals Christine and her family who had finally made it to Bognor Regis. They were allocated to a group which was taken to a bungalow on Pagham beach. The chalet became a temporary home for three families consisting of 'three mothers and eleven children and fourteen cans of corned beef'. Conditions were not ideal, but rather than going home Christine's family found themselves better accommodation consisting of two Victorian railway carriages.

At a reception centre in Effingham, Surrey, five busloads of distraught and homesick evacuees pulled to a stop outside the dance hall and catering establishment that belonged to Martin's mother. It felt like 'a bit of an invasion' but Martin pitched in to help 'these poor evacuees'. While some were being fed, others were being entertained, and many were being cleaned up in the official de-lousing centre of Martin's garden shed. In Horsham, evacuees arrived in the little Sussex town where 'many people from very different backgrounds and for a variety of reasons', including homelessness, descended upon Frank's house. Two families of Jewish tailors, 'formidably British to the core and I think if Hitler had known about them, he would have given up', moved in and commuted daily to London's blitzed East End, and later a Jewish refugee arrived: 'He was about eleven years old and his name was Max. Max used to goose-step with the other boys around the breakfast room shouting, "Heil Hitler." Much time was spent looking for the hat which he wore at mealtimes but frequently hidden by the other boys.'

In Dartmouth, 'a trainload of dishevelled, frightened, tearful children' arrived and were lined up on the Town Hall steps for inspection and collection. Nine-year-old June was allowed to stay up late to watch this scene at the Town Hall from the balcony of her billet, but to her it seemed 'a harrowing experience' and she was relieved she was not in the shoes of those children. Technically she was, but she was a private evacuee. For some children there was little difference between an evacuee on the National Evacuation Scheme and a private evacuee: one was billeted with total strangers and the other with virtual strangers. Phyl was a private evacuee, having been evacuated to her grandmother, and to her it conferred a totally different standing in comparison to the National evacuees. When the local schoolchildren referred to her and her siblings as 'only evacuees', Phyl was quick to protest in self-defence that she was a 'private and not your common or garden sort'. Being privately evacuated did confer one big advantage over the National evacuees: they did not have to go through the public selection process.

When children arrived in their reception areas, the solution to locating a billet for each child was to invite the potential foster carers to a communal selection viewing. This enabled fosterers to scrutinise, hand-pick and take home a child of their particular choice. It was certainly a critical moment as matches were made that could make or break the whole evacuation experience, and everything depended on that first impression. This process of selection proved to be an unhappy memory for many child evacuees. Even John, whose evacuation was running efficiently, faltered at the selection process as he found that being paraded in front of strangers who 'eyed us up and down' was 'very embarrassing'. Little Ronald stood stiffly to attention in a school hall in Measham, Leicestershire, where he found it hard to understand what the locals were saying and they did not appear to understand him either. He was very unhappy at being examined by potential foster parents because he and his classmates were 'in many cases poorly dressed, from the working class districts of Birmingham, who in many cases were terrified' and that 'dignity was in short supply'. Ronald's sister and brothers were quickly picked and spirited away to different villages and he, at the tender age of six, was now all on his own, the last of his siblings to be chosen. He would later recall the scene as being like 'a cattle or even a slave market' and was something he could 'never forget'.

Pamela from West London was in a real cattle market. She had arrived at Bletchley, Buckinghamshire and unhappily waited with the rest of her school to be transferred to another village. She found the whole experience of the unfamiliar a 'traumatic experience'. Eight-year-old Joan from Deptford, south-east London, sat in a school hall in Northamptonshire, tired, hungry and wanting her mother. When 'people started coming in to choose who they wanted we felt like sheep waiting to be picked out'. Londoner John trudged the pavements of a village with a bedraggled group, walking from house to house to find a billet and feeling as if whole process was 'not unlike the slave trade in reverse'.

An alternative selection method was this door-to-door approach where children, some of whom had been travelling all day, were taken around the village or town, knocking on doors in search of people who would take them in. Trevor in Ditton, Kent, met a bus-load of evacuees, all of who were under the age of eleven from London's East End, each one labelled and carrying their gas masks and belongings in cases or wrapped in brown paper and tied with string. With the vicar and policeman in the lead and village boys helping carry cases, they all set off down the road knocking on doors of those households who had spare room. The villagers did not have a choice as to whether they wanted to take in an evacuee, which was why the policeman was there: 'Of course some people objected but the policeman said it was the law and the children went in.' Trevor carried the case of a ten-year-old girl and her little brother. The pair must have looked as if they had suffered deprivations because the lady who opened her door to them 'burst into tears as she gathered them up. Ditton was a poor village then and the children were very poor.'

Someone was always going to be the very last one chosen and that would leave an indelible memory on those who would never forget that feeling of being the least wanted. One ten-year-old girl arrived somewhere in the depths of the Lake District to be 'herded into a large hall where people came and chose a child then left'. She found herself and her brother to be the very last two remaining. That mattered very much to her: 'I looked out of the window saying fiercely to myself, "I don't care if no-one wants me, I don't care." I had never felt so unwanted in my life.' Londoner Charles, who had by now bleakly realized he was not actually on holiday, faced the village hall selection process where 'some foster parents took one child with them and quickly departed with their "prize" whilst others took as many as three or four'. One potential fosterer requested, within hearing of the small band of boys in Charles's group, 'Two clean girls from nice homes.' Charles's friends tried 'to look angelic so they would get picked' which appeared to work as suddenly only Charles and one other boy remained, and being last was an awful feeing: 'I choked back the tears as I realized just how alone I was and to this day, the personal loneliness of that time has never, thank God!, been repeated.'

An eight-year-old from London arrived in a hall in Brighton, his face brown with chocolate as he had been stealthily eating the large bar from his ration bag. Foster parents came and went, choosing their evacuees. Firstly 'the better dressed girls' were selected, 'followed by the remaining girls, then the better dressed boys' until there were just five children left – 'the dregs of the earth'. It did not seem to bother the boy as he was far more concerned that he might be told off for eating all that chocolate. With no more volunteer foster parents in the hall, there was no other option for the billeting officers than to scrub the boy's face clean with a floor cloth and set off door to door until someone, somewhere, decided to have him. He was not the only boy to have an unpromising start to his evacuation experience. Young David, newly fatherless and homeless, arrived in Cornwall after a seemingly endless train journey and found himself in the growing darkness of the evening being driven to his billet by the local undertaker; an inauspicious start.

Nine-year-old Irene travelled with the Sherwood Park Infants School evacuees, teddy bear in hand and a hand-made white canvas bag of belongings slung over her shoulder. It was dark when she finally left the local hall in Egham, Staines, to be placed at her billet. Her foster parent looked surprised when she saw the nice clothes in Irene's bag, obviously expecting that 'children from London would be poorly dressed as, indeed, some of them were, often arriving in layers of all the clothes they possessed, and sometimes very dirty'. Charles would later reflect that people in reception areas had 'preconceived ideas of London children being delinquent, dirty and unruly, who had never seen a cow or green fields and would not be able to cope with the culture shock . . . these dead-end kids'.

It came as a shock to John in Colchester when he saw real poverty first-hand when the evacuees, mainly mothers and small children, arrived: 'I had been poor for most of my life, but the poverty I witnessed then with these poor mothers and babies plucked from the slums of the East End of London, horrified me. I remember some poor little girl tripped and fell in the hall and I saw she was naked under her thin cotton frock. Well, I always had a clean pair of pants, they may have been a bit ragged but I had some (and they were clean every week, changed after a bath on Saturday night; that was considered perfectly adequate in those days).' A rural vicar took one look at the child evacuees from London who had arrived to invade his parish and promptly ordered the village policeman to put them straight back on the next train to Paddington; the policeman complied.[2]

During the second wave of evacuation in 1940, Croydon boy Colin discovered that there was bias towards Londoners incurred from the first wave of evacuation: 'I found out later, the local people had said, "No more children from London. The first ones were terrible!" That was why there were so few ladies willing to take us. Also it was the reason that I heard the teachers telling the ladies that we had come from "nice" families.' Another London boy, who was a knowledgeable evacuee as he had been through this process three times already, summed up his experiences in five words: 'Basically we were not wanted.' In his opinion, 'the vast majority of foster parents didn't feel sorry for the plight of the children away from their parents'. He also felt that 'those in the country thought all city children were criminals' and that evacuees were seen as either an income because of their billeting allowance, or as a potential source of free labour. Richard was one of those London evacuees who was taken door to door to find a billet, tired, dazed and upset, while the exasperated adult a 'good works' woman tried valiantly to convince villagers to take them in. He had not eaten anything that day but he was in such despair that he felt he 'would never be hungry again'. It was growing dark, but 'nobody wanted London boys, we had an imagined reputation. Too much

Dickens, too much Artful Dodger Syndrome in this small town.'

Poverty and preconceptions were not just confined to children from London. The MP for Glasgow, Mr Buchanan, vigorously defended Glasgow's evacuees when comments about their verminous state were aired in the House of Commons. Reports had been heard from more than one constituency about the horrors of filthy, disease-ridden Glaswegians with 'indescribable' habits descending on unsuspecting billets.[3] Evacuees from Liverpool were also much maligned. Apparently, householders in Wales who had billeted Liverpool evacuees had to burn bedding, clothing, curtains and blinds to fumigate their homes afterwards, and in one case an entire bedroom had to be completely stripped after resident evacuees had used it as a toilet.[4] In a Nottinghamshire village the first lot of evacuees came from Sheffield and they caused some consternation. A neighbour knocked on the door of eight-year-old Olive's house in quite a state as 'two girls had been delivered to her home, and what they stood up in was just rags' and she had called to beg some clothes for them. The next lot to arrive were 'equally poverty-stricken children from Great Yarmouth'. Another knock on another door, this time at Mary's house in Haworth, was to ask Mary's mother to inspect the Bradford evacuees because it was discovered they were riddled with head lice. The paucity and difference in lifestyle of some, but not all, of the Bradford children was evident when 'some of the evacuees refused to go in the bath' and 'at weekends some of the parents came over with bottles of beer and didn't pay much attention to their children, but sat around drinking beer'. The Bradford evacuee boy billeted with Mary's neighbour was, however, 'spotlessly clean'.

> 'Here are your two evacuees.' 'Don't want them.' 'But you signed the form.' 'Yes, but I didn't expect that there would be a war.' What a welcome!
>
> Stanley Sloop

From the poor welcome at a billet in Brighton where their prospective foster-father made it clear that evacuees were the last thing he wanted on his doorstep, things did not improve for Londoner Stanley and his twin: 'It was a very unhappy stay as the likes of us were not allowed to eat with the family. We had to eat in the kitchen with the dog'. Fortunately they soon moved. Unfortunately it was to a house with a case of TB, but there were signs of better times ahead when they received a warm welcome at their third billet where they remained until their return to London which, they were assured, 'wasn't going to be bombed'. They got home just in time for the Blitz.

Alan faced a similar scenario on his second evacuation. In 1944 he landed in South Yorkshire and it was not the most promising of starts: 'Brother and I dumped on the doorstep, in the dark, of a house in Waleswood. No idea where our sisters were. It was dark and it was late. The house was empty but the door was unlocked. Sat there for some time until a merry couple arrived and greeted us with "what the #### do you want." They had forgotten that they had promised to take evacuees. It was the first time that I had heard the 'F' word from an adult.' Fortunately the boys were re-billeted to Kiveton Park, separately though, where Alan's brother had a great billet with a charming couple. Regrettably, Alan was to find that he was living in a dysfunctional household with 'a wife beater' so he was quickly moved again, this time to an overcrowded miner's cottage where he had to share a double bed in a tiny bedroom with 'a crazy old man everyone in the street called the Colonel'. On the plus side, the food was good and he got taken to football matches.

Children's experience of evacuation was dependant not just on each child's personality and background, but whether they were lucky enough to get a billet that could make them feel at home. Michael was really happy with his foster carers in Burnley, Lancashire, and was soon calling them Auntie and Uncle. Edwin, who was treasured and 'treated like Little Lord Fauntleroy' in his billet, was astounded by the kindness and generosity of his foster parents: 'I was given a birthday party, a football and football boots. I had never had anything but a custard or cocoa tin, cigarette cards and lead soldiers which were repaired forever with bits of matchstick to put arms, legs and heads back on with.' His sisters, billeted separately from their brother, were not quite as comfortable in their new home after they discovered their foster mother had a fondness for popping out her glass eye, something the younger sister never quite got used to.

Edwin and his sisters had a second evacuation, this time to 'the land of Lorna Doone' on the Somerset and Devon border where their foster parents once again 'showered us with great affection and love'. Another happy boy was Eric who was billeted at a farm. Being a townie it was the first time he had ever seen a farm and life was about to be very different from his home in a middle-class area of Newcastle with his reasonably affluent parents. He had the good fortune to be chosen by a 'cheerful, hard-working couple' where he was fully accepted as a member of the family. He was one happy boy from the start. Farm life, totally different to what he had ever known, really suited him and he fully embraced every aspect of country lifestyle: 'What exciting days they were.' Making her evacuees feel at home was important to David's kindly foster carer and consequently he was really happy: '. . . no one could have been more caring, it must have been very hard on her having to look after us two rascals'. One boy in his first billet felt really well taken care off as he received 'better care and was better dressed' than he had been at home. In Yorkshire, Margaret positively embraced the company of the evacuee girl who was billeted with them: '. . . we could actually do things together, and it was nice to have someone else to talk to'.

Unfortunately, not every child was billeted in a suitable place. Viv had a difficult start on her first evacuation in 1944, and it only got worse. Her mother had desperately traipsed around the village in Staffordshire for hours searching for someone to take in her seven-year-old daughter. Finally, a farmer's wife who only wanted a boy evacuee as a friend for her son was persuaded to reluctantly take Viv after her conscience was pricked with tales of London's V1 attacks. For Viv, who was never going to measure up to her foster brother's expectations as she was a girl, it was far from ideal: 'And so my trials began.' As her mother waved goodbye, Viv felt 'panic and a sense of loss'. Long, lonely days of bullying and homesickness began. Some children were so unhappy in their billets that they ran away. Colin from

Croydon, back in the newly opened Cypress Road School which had returned from a short stint in Brighton, listened wide-eyed to the horror stories told by returning friends, some of who 'had a very bad time'. Rumour had it that two girls ran away from their Brighton billet all the way home to Croydon.

In contrast to farm-loving Eric, a twelve-year-old boy from Coventry found it very hard to settle in with a farm worker's family in Warwickshire, though he conceded that it was not their fault as he was 'an only child and had led a sheltered life at home, "mammy licked" we used to call it'. One London family was not having the best experience of farm life either as they were forced to live in a cow shed. After hearing of this family's living conditions, evacuee Robert accompanied his headmaster father and a billeting officer to a farmhouse outside Pencader, mid-Wales, to investigate. They found a mother and three young children billeted in a 'draughty, damp empty cowshed . . . wind blew in from the missing door and window openings'. The large farmhouse was occupied by a 'house-proud and nervous' widow who, peering through her window at these foreigners from London, decided that the semi-derelict barn was more than fit for purpose. A family from the docklands of London were accommodated in the stable block of Hillingdon House in Essex, home of one boy's grandfather. The evacuees appeared perfectly happy living in the horses' looseboxes for a number of years during the war as no expense had been spared on the construction of the stables: 'Comfort for horses came high on my grandfather's list of priorities.'

In Scotland, the Duke of Argyll did not appear to welcome evacuees in his large, multi-bedroom castle on the shore of Loch Fyne. The 150 women and children that arrived in Inverary camped in the town hall on paltry bedding made from straw-filled sacks and dirty mattresses acquired from the local prison. There were only two toilets in the whole building. The Duke eventually conceded to take in a few children; it was claimed he confined them to the castle basements. While the people of Inverary tried to do their best to help the evacuees, no arrangements appeared to have been made for billeting. An

Episcopal minister offered a place for two teachers, but only after he had pulled up the carpet in the room first. The rest of the evacuees were given condemned houses to live in.[5]

The difficulties faced by children as they adapted to different habits and lifestyles in their new world could be challenging. Viv struggled with the table etiquette at her billet: 'They couldn't believe it when I chewed a mouthful of potato or porridge before swallowing it, and I in my turn stared in amazement as food disappeared down their throats as if it were liquid', and she tried hard to master the art of eating without apparently chewing. An eight-year-old boy also had a problem with the food at his first billet where his foster father, a retired army man who had served in India, had a penchant for curry. Wednesday night was curry night, and the boy hated curry. Nevertheless, curry nights aside, he was better fed than he had been at home. Derek tried to get used to the custom at his billet: '. . . completely foreign to me, supper was a proper sit down meal'. Sunday dinner at Charles' billet was a chore he would rather not have had to endure. Pride of place on the table every Sunday was a pig's head complete with an apple stuffed in its mouth. The pig was carved and served by the head of the house with the two evacuee boys being served last, not that Charles minded as he recoiled from his dinner: 'I often prayed that he would miss me altogether.'

Cleone and her mother were placed with 'a large family who lived in a council house built to replace the slum dwellings' where life was a little different to what they were used to. Apart from finding that the family kept coal in the bath, Cleone was horrified when they 'ate their Yorkshire pudding with gravy before the main course. I hated Yorkshire pudding and thought this was all we were going to get.' Head lice were the last straw and forced Cleone and her mother to move. In the headmaster's house in Watchet, Maurice also felt uncomfortably out of place because of social differences: it was 'quite posh'. He was not used to having a whole bedroom to himself, or of having to wash his hands before meals and having to go to bed at 7pm. 'It was all very strange to me . . . their middle class background was not the same as I was used to.' Happily for him, he soon moved on to the house of the village postman where he settled in and had 'much more freedom and no more church on Sunday'.

Charles from Liverpool also found his billet in Leek to be greatly different from home. It took him a moment to get over 'the shock of feeling carpet' beneath his feet, and being greeted with the words, 'Whenever you come into the house in future you must use the back door only, and take your boots off before you come in.' The gleaming, immaculate furniture, the luxury of a private bedroom complete with wardrobe, dressing table and bedside light, was almost as astonishing as the pristine white bath with hot running water straight out of a tap – so very different from a scrub in a tin bath in front of the fire. Luxury it may have been, but for an adventurous boy used to the excitement of wartime Liverpool it was nothing more than unbearable 'confinement'. A begging letter home to his mother set into motion Charles's happy relocation to a billet that had '"home" dripping from its every crowded corner'.

Sleeping in a strange house could also be the source of discomfort for child evacuees, though for evacuee Jill it was the quietness of a village after the constant noise of a city that was the problem: 'I couldn't sleep at first because of the silence.' For some, it was the sleeping arrangements that caused the biggest issues. Muriel was happy at her billet in Trimley St. Mary, but after only six weeks she had to move again to join her grammar school, Palmer's College, and in her new billet there arose the problem of sharing a bed. Muriel's foster parents were really kind but she found it unbearable to endure sleepless nights sharing a tiny bed with their daughter who ground her teeth, continuously, all night. A heartfelt letter to her mother, 'please bring me home', all written in kisses, resulted in her swift return. Muriel was not the only child to have issues with sleeping arrangements. Richard was made to not only share a room with another evacuee boy, but to share a bed with him too. Poor Richard remained as stoical as an unhappy nine-year-old could be by justifying his plight: 'I had never known such misery, but it was war.'

In London-boy Charles' billet, he and his friend Andy experienced difficulty sleeping in the attic with its ominous view of the young offenders Borstal Institution, plus they were very uncomfortable in the cold, damp, ancient bed. It did not help that they had been 'gleefully' told by their foster parents' sons that the old lady whose bed it had been had actually died in it. Charles, thoroughly homesick, was crying into his pillow one night when poor Andy next to him, who was equally unhappy, accidently wet the bed. This caused their foster mother 'to wonder if all evacuees "leaked at both ends when they went to bed?"' Frank from Eastbourne was also made to share a bed. Squeezed into a farm cottage near Abbots Langley along with four other evacuees, they were all made to sleep like sardines 'in the same double bed, sideways on'. He suspected his foster parents were taking as many evacuees as possible to make a 'profit from the system'. The upside was that the evacuees were all 'allowed to run riot', and live a little boys' dream whereby they 'stayed in bed as long as we liked, played around the fields where the husband was a farm worker, scrumped apples from the orchards, and were generally completely undisciplined'. The only intervention from their foster mother was the once weekly delousing treatment and a regular dose of laxatives. One little four-year-old girl had the greatest predicament, also sharing a double bed but with not one, or four, but several other evacuees. They all slept 'top and tail with boys and girls all in together' and 'it was not surprising that among these small children incontinence problems were experienced and it does not leave a lot to the imagination to guess just what the environment was like, especially as quite often the sheets were just dried by the fire and put back on the bed'.

The sleeping arrangements were much better in Derek and his brother's billet, a two-up-two-down terraced house in Wolverhampton. The local authority there had provided each child with a camp bed and two blankets in addition to the monetary allowance per child. Beneath their L.A camp beds squatted the customary chamber pots, an all-important piece of equipment necessary to save that night-time trek to the outside privy. One nine-year-old boy, Edwin, discovered with delight that when he threw himself onto the bed in his billet for the first time, it was like 'falling onto clouds'. This was a feather bed. All to himself. For a boy used to sleeping three to a bed at home, he was in heaven. At least they had beds to sleep in, unlike six-year-old Daniel from West Ham whose billet in St Ives, Cornwall, did not have room for him so he ended up sleeping 'on a mattress on a board on the bath'. Eventually he was moved into another billet but fared no better there as his foster mother had a beach café and had taken on 'sixteen London evacuees as cheap labour', profiteering even more than Frank's fosterers.

> *There were twenty or so of us. Odd Bods, Misfits, Wet the Beds,*
> *Tearaways and Runaways.*
>
> R. Berger

As an evacuee, a child's role in a billet could be quite different from home and some foster parents took advantage of an extra pair of hands. Betty from South London was treated more like a governess and housekeeper rather than one of the family. She had to instruct her foster brothers in maths, and her chores were to do 'the washing up, clean shoes, do the shopping in the local town on Saturday mornings, polish and dust in the afternoons. Of course there was often darning in the afternoons.' One little six-year-old girl was 'expected to help with the housework which sometimes included black-leading the kitchen range' and every evening, including in the bitterly cold winter, to scrub the stone scullery floor before bed. It was quite the opposite for Jean at Farley Green near Guildford. She was delighted that she had no chores to do at her billet. Her foster carer 'didn't believe in making us do things if we didn't want to', a situation which naturally made Jean feel she was 'in clover'.

One boy was unlikely to be embracing his role in his latest billet. By the time London was experiencing the V1s, he was no longer in his first billet in Brighton. At the age of thirteen he was in fact in billet No. 6, having absconded from billets Nos. 4 and 5. The first time he left through boredom and ran away back home, and the second time he escaped a foster carer who was too liberal with the cane and therefore he attempted to walk from Chertsey, Surry, to Wales – a safer option than facing the wrath of Mother and the doodlebugs. There were about twenty boys in his billet No. 6, 'a home for naughty boys', and his job was to wake the bed-wetters up for the bathroom during the night. He was not the only boy to find himself in an evacuee hostel for wayward boys. Twenty-six 'difficult" evacuee boys were plucked from their billets in valleys west of Salisbury to be interred in a house provided by Portsmouth Council.[6] By the summer of 1943, a total of 224 hostels for 'difficult' children housed nearly 3,500 children. Residents included those exhibiting 'maladjustment" (bed wetting, disobedience or troublesome behaviour) or 'neurotics' (sleep disturbances, crying or anxiety) or delinquents. Some had medical needs such as asthma.[7]

Little Terry only spent one night at his first billet. As soon as it was found that he was registered as having asthma he was immediately moved to the evacuee hostel of Island House in Loughborough. With twenty-three other boys he spent fifteen months in an unheated, bare-floored building with just three members of staff. All the hostel boys were allocated jobs such as chopping wood, and fingers 'but that was par for the course'. Little Terry worked in the stable block which was a bonus as he could help himself to the horses' carrots to supplement his food. Permanently hungry, he resorted to nibbling on his Gibbs Toothpaste blocks to alleviate hunger pangs. The hostel had a strict regime where 'the ultimate penalty for transgressions was to be sent to bed, possibly after a beating with the Matron's stick'. A punishment for being too noisy one day saw all the boys locked in the cellar, lights off. The worst punishment that little Terry was forced to endure was a beating followed by two days' cleaning an outside toilet whilst repeatedly being told he would never be allowed to see his parents again.

Billets aside, fitting in with the local community was another key factor to a successful evacuation. With most children having had little experience of the world outside their own neighbourhood, a different county might as well be a foreign country, especially if they could not understand a word of what the locals were saying. There were some rocky starts. While Ronald from Birmingham struggled with the Leicestershire accent, John, a self-confessed 'fully embedded

Cockney' from Hungary, found 'the Wiltshire burr . . . quite foreign'. Another London boy discovered his foster mother had a 'very pronounced Wiltshire accent', but soon he discovered he had too. As Irene was from London, she was 'certainly expected to have a cockney accent', and seven-year-old evacuee Viv got teased in Staffordshire for her London accent so she learnt 'to say boozz instead of bus pretty quickly and soon had a passable Staffordshire twang'. The first words eight-year-old Londoner Emily uttered to her foster mother was, 'Missus, where's the Dyke?' which Emily realized was 'not a good start'. Before too long, Emily's foster mother wrote to the child's mother to say she was promptly sending her home. Seeing as Emily, her four siblings and parents were technically homeless and living in various reception centres in the bombed-out docklands of London, there was not actually a home to return to.

On his first evacuation Alan might as well have been in a foreign country as far as he was concerned as he was in Stansted where 'everyone spoke like Walter Gabriel'. Five years later he found himself even further away from home and was having difficulties living in the alien world of Yorkshire where 'this time they all spoke like Wilfred Pickles'. His 'feeling of complete alienation' was not helped by being 'given a light duffing-up' in a derelict air-raid shelter by some local boys. Wales presented a challenge as evacuees not only had to cope with a different accent in Wales, but the Welsh language too. One little boy returned to the outskirts of London from his evacuation in Wales only for his older brother to be completely unable to understand a single word he said as he was speaking Welsh, and Robert heard of twins who returned 'home to London at the end of the war, to greet their mystified parents in Welsh; they had altogether lost their English'.

In Wales, some evacuees from big cities felt distinctly out of place, such as when 414 mothers and children from Liverpool arrived in the tiny village of Aberdaron. Two weeks later only fifty remained.[8] Robert was a London boy yet even he could appreciate the difficulties fellow Londoners had in rural Wales. It was not an easy transition on either side: 'The locals cannot have found it easy to cope with these disorientated Londoners.' The London evacuees appeared to be struggling to settle into the small, quiet community of Pencader. These refugees – mothers and children – were seen frequently 'wandering desperately around the village' in the persistent Welsh rain, 'wondering whatever to do', and the children who were 'used to running about in the streets all day . . . were quite unused to chapel on Sundays'. The social hub in the village was centred on Pencader's small fish and chip shop where business was booming. At this collective meeting point, 'people would pass the time of day there, as they chewed their two penn'orth or four penn'orth of chips, and deliberated over the amount of vinegar'. One pair of evacuees was so disenchanted with rural Wales that they attempted to return to the familiarity of the London bombing and set off walking. 'Unfortunately they chose the wrong direction, and were found near Aberystwyth, nearly forty miles further into darkest Wales'.

Of course there were those who delighted in the freedom of the Welsh valleys. Bill and Bob, the Isleworth boys now known as 'those Damn Vaccies in Dowlais', not only settled in but improved greatly in health. In London they both had their legs in braces due to having rickets, but with all the fresh air and food in the valleys they 'shed their irons in Wales and learn to run and play with the rest of the children'. The boys quickly picked up choice words of the local language from their Welsh friends, '. . . and as quickly as possible unlearnt it as it was scrubbed from their tongues with carbolic soap'. Surrey girl Jill spent a happy evacuation in Builth Wells where she was safe. When her parents came to visit her it was with fortuitous timing – their Surrey home was destroyed by a doodlebug while they were away.

Successful integration with the local community was important if new friendships were going to be formed. In some cases, evacuees from different backgrounds mixed in really well. In fact, Charles from Liverpool found that the boys and girls at Ashbourne Road School, Leek, were 'a really good crowd and we had great fun together', and in addition the local children of Ball Haye Green had 'taken to us strangers from Liverpool and Manchester to their hearts'. They exchanged tales of city air raids and farm life, and 'it was as if we were family already'. Charles and his brother were so enjoying their new community that when their father arrived out of the blue to take them home, it was a 'bombshell'. Alan had felt very much the outsider when he was evacuated to Yorkshire but his status completely changed when his sporting success altered his social standing from stranger to local celebrity. He discovered the sport of boxing at a youth club, and he was remarkably good at it. Winning a boxing match in Sheffield was 'a turning point in coping with . . . life as an evacuee'. Elevated in status, Alan could now 'walk the walk and talk the talk in the village'.

I arrived back in London as the Blitz began and bombs were raining down nightly, but who cared now. I was home.

Richard Reeve

Homesickness was very common for a lot of children and in some cases it was the cause of evacuees returning home much sooner than expected. Maurice's homecoming was typical as it was initiated by him. He was homesick, 'this country life is not for me', and he wrote repeatedly to his mother to please come and get him until she finally relented. Eastender Evelyn and her cousin were brought home by their mothers for a very different reason. Their foster mother had written saying she would like to keep the girls and could she adopt them. Panicked, the girls' mothers rushed to Wales and retrieved their children immediately. During Richard's evacuation he was aware that many of the London children had gone back home and he saw this as children being 'rescued by parents who missed them too much'. He had to wait until he had won a scholarship to grammar school before his mother came to liberate him, and he returned home just in time for the London Blitz, but he did not care about the bombing as the most important thing for him was 'I was home'.

Though some children coped well with evacuation, others did not. For many, the whole period of evacuation was a time of uncertainty and upheaval. The feeling of being 'taken away from everything familiar in our young lives' and not fully comprehending why, left Pamela in a perpetual state of 'wondering if we would ever see our families again'. No one sat Pamela down to enlighten her as 'it was not thought necessary in those days to explain anything to children. No one understood we had rights or feelings. We just had to do as we were told or be punished.' While the whole experience was influenced by factors such as the background and personality of each child, receiving appropriate support from family and foster carers was very important in helping children cope with being away from home. When that support system failed, the results could be devastating.

One child, a four-year-old boy, had a traumatic evacuation. He was evacuated with his South London boarding school and did not see his mother for eighteen months, by which time her traumatised son 'could only speak in a whisper and had a dreadful stammer'. Seventy years later he was still inclined to stammer under stress which to him was 'proof that early childhood experiences remain for life'. One of the most disturbing cases was that of two small boys, Peter and his brother, both under the age of five. They were evacuated from Surrey to a reputedly respectable billet in Wallasey. Overstretched officials who did not follow procedures failed to allocate the boys a medical officer, and the billet received no inspection from child protection services. During the boys' evacuation Peter's brother died, reputedly from natural causes. Later, Peter was later admitted to hospital suffering from 'shock and maltreatment'. The foster carers were fined in court.[9]

For those children who were strongly affected by their wartime experiences, access to professional services was through the Child Guidance Clinics (CGC). The psychological effects of evacuation on schoolchildren were acknowledged by the Board of Education who helped fund the sixty-two CGC situated in reception areas in 1942.[10] But help was not always readily available. In the reception area of Huntingdon no funds were available to employ a child psychologist despite a request being made to Women's Voluntary Service (WVS) headquarters. It was only by appealing to people they knew in America that WVS supporters could raise enough money to employ a psychologist in Huntingdon, and then only for the limited period of three months. Within the first six months of war, 142 children in the county of Huntingdonshire were recognized as needing professional counselling. The majority of these were evacuees.[11]

Although the transition from home to billet could be a difficult time, the return home could be every bit as challenging. Viv never felt wanted in her foster home. Unbeknown to her parents she was desperately unhappy and felt unable to tell them. After eighteen months she returned home but the transition was just as difficult. Her homecoming was 'dominated by the shock of seeing a bomb site opposite our house', and though relieved to be home she felt reticent, unable to bring herself to talk about her evacuation and the effect it had on her. At the beginning of little Jo's evacuation it had taken many weeks for her to understand that she was not 'going home on Monday' and she suffered repeated nightmares that her mother and baby brother died in a gas attack. But during her long years of evacuation she settled into her new life and was happy, until the day it came to an abrupt end. For Jo, going home was a disturbing event and the arrival of her mother and aunt, 'these people who I could scarcely remember', made her feel as if her 'world again was turned upside down'. Returning to Birmingham was a difficult transition made worse by her feelings of alienation: 'It was all very strange and I was completely lost and bewildered. People I didn't know came to look at the returned evacuee. My brothers looked at me with great suspicion; my sister was off-hand. I was six when I left and twelve and a half when I returned.'

The effects of prolonged lack of contact with family were far-reaching. 'Billet-bind', a condition where the billet and foster carer's become the only home and family a child really knew, caused difficult homecomings. One little girl received only one visit from her mother in all of her six years of being an evacuee. Having not seen her mother since the age of four, she stood 'on the little station platform . . . with absolutely no idea of who I was meeting or what she would look like'. As a consequence, she did not experience homesickness until she actually returned home when she found herself yearning for the one home she remembered – her billet. Another child, aged nine at the end of her evacuation, felt distraught at having to leave her billet in a Somerset village because after five years it had become home: 'I knew [the end of war] meant I would be going back to London, and I really didn't want to'. Even older children experienced difficulty leaving the lives they had lived as evacuees. Sheena and her sister Nancy, evacuated on the CORB scheme, had settled so well into their new lives in Canada that when they returned home in 1945 as 'two strangers', neither were 'able to get onto the same family footing with our parents as we had before the war'.

Alan did not experience billet-bind but his evacuation experience caused rifts between him and his family. Throughout his first evacuation, which lasted three years, he strongly felt a widening gap between his life before and his life then: 'My home, my school friends, my father who visited about once a month on his bicycle and even my mother, drifted from me, and family life, for me, never recovered.' He felt very much for his mother who had 'a wretched time . . . trying to keep some sort of contact with her other three children who were gradually growing up and drifting away from her'. Alan's second evacuation saw him separated from his siblings and mother for yet another year and the family bonds grew ever more tenuous. He felt depressed while he counted down the days until the end of the war and his return home. It proved to be 'a very long year' which would leave 'scars on all of us'. Returning home was just as difficult as waiting to go home: 'When it came and I returned home with my brother and sister, who by now I hardly knew, to a school where I was re-joining a class where nobody else seemed to have been away, and where I alone was the returning evacuee, I felt I had been the victim of a gigantic confidence trick and I don't think I ever forgave my parents.'

In contrast, many children experienced positive evacuations where there was no trauma, no feelings of isolation or regret. Derek had only been away a short while but he would always remember his foster carers for a memorable act of kindness. His foster-father gave him a farewell present, a bicycle, which he had shipped by train to Derek's home in Banstead. Eric enjoyed every minute of his evacuation between the ages of eleven and fourteen on a farm in Cumberland. He became part of their 'family unit' and this experience left him with some treasured childhood memories. Edwin, evacuated with his sisters, would be forever thankful for his foster carers in both of his billets for 'looking after us and giving us a life that we would otherwise never have known'. Happy evacuations would never be forgotten and in some cases the ties would remain for a lifetime. During their evacuation, Michael and his younger sister formed a strong bond with their elderly foster carers and they kept in touch with the couple until they died. In Crayford, Kent, Christine wrote a letter to the teacher of the school in Lancashire where she spent a short, unsettled evacuation. That letter was to be the first of many, written almost every week without fail for the next fifty-seven years.

Charles from Liverpool would always remember his happy days as an evacuee in Leek and would one day make 'a pilgrimage' back there to meet his foster parents' son to 'thank him personally for what his parents had done for me during the war'. Daniel was left with the fondest memories of his third and final evacuation at the age of ten in a billet in Yorkshire at the home of a coal miner and his wife. They were 'the epitome of kindly folk reaching out a hand to those in trouble'. Fourteen years later he became a life-long member of the caring family by marrying their granddaughter. In Grace's village of Elston, one evacuee boy who was billeted with a childless couple effectively became the son they never had: '. . . he stayed, and they left him the cottage. He married and brought up a family in that cottage.' Cleone and her family remained in their reception area of Halstead. They made it their home not just for the duration of the war but for the next seventeen years. The nine-year-old girl who was distraught at leaving her Somerset billet for a half-remembered home in London would one day write her wartime memoirs as a seventy-year-old woman from her home, her Somerset home.

Chapter 4

Invasion

My parents were regarded with some suspicion by a few people in Otley. I wondered if it was because of my father's moustache (which may have reminded people of Hitler) . . .

Julia Woledge

A German invasion of Britain was a very real possibility in 1940, and the prospect of being captured by the enemy evoked some dramatic reactions. David's father believed there was only one solution should the enemy invade. He prepared his son for his fate: 'From his chest of drawers he took a black Bakelite box which had a green lid. In the box he showed me a hypodermic syringe and some ampoules of morphine. He said, "If Hitler invades this country I will put you out." I was about seven years old.'

In Surrey, eight-year-old Jill was conscious that certain plans were being made in her household: 'There was some pact or understanding between my parents, that should my father be taken away or killed if occupied by the Germans, that my mother, sister and I would take our own lives – how, I have no idea – I think tablets.' Jill was not afraid of this; to her mind this was what happened in war. Barbara was well aware of what her mother was planning after she had overheard her passionately declaring that she would kill the whole family rather than let the Germans take them. Unlike Jill, Barbara was not too happy with the thought of that, deciding that she would instead 'run away from home rather than submit to such a fate'. She was determined to 'find my own way of resisting the Germans'. Another young girl, Patricia, also overheard a conversation, this time between her mother and her mother's friend who firmly stated that 'if the Germans ever got as far as Hounslow, her daughter's head was going in the gas oven'. Patricia took a while to work out the meaning of that and when she did she very much hoped that her mother did not have the same solution.

In Bournemouth, Mary Lou's mother took a different stance. She meant for her family to survive come what may and took practical steps to ensure they did: 'There was always the worry of food shortage and my prudent mother hung many tins of food among the thick branches of the large trees we had in the garden, in case there was an invasion.' Regrettably, her mother forgot to take into account the typical British weather and therefore 'when it rained it washed off most of the labels, so after the war it was hit and miss whether we cut down a tin of processed peas or peaches'. In Dunstable, people were 'in a defiant frame of mind' and were 'going to give Hitler a bloody nose if he crossed the Channel', while in Salisbury one father was well prepared to defend his family: 'My father kept a long stick embedded with nails behind the kitchen door and said it was for any Nazi who walked down our garden. Shades of *Dad's Army*.'

German parachutists could be anywhere, at any place, at any time. Barbara did her bit by keeping her eyes peeled for spies as 'the fevered atmosphere of the expected invasion and strong anti-German feelings produced rumours of spies being dropped in all sorts of guises'. She specifically looked for nuns and if she found any she planned to surreptitiously inspect their boots. Nuns wearing German Para boots would certainly raise suspicions. Elsewhere, pony club members rode their ponies around the countryside on parachute patrol, ready to relay reports at a gallop should an enemy land.[1] They were wise to be cautious as German secret agents and saboteurs did in fact parachute into Britain and Ireland. One spy unfortunately parachuted straight into the murky waters of the Manchester Ship Canal and drowned.[2] Two were caught in Scotland after giving themselves away by cycling on the wrong side of the road, and a search of their cases revealed tell-tale German sausage and Nivea hand cream (made in Hamburg).[3] When thirty-six German bodies washed up on the coasts of southern England over a six-week period at the end of a tense summer, it was believed that that they were part of an attempted invasion force. On 7 September the invasion alert of 'Cromwell' was issued by General Headquarters of the Home Forces, an action which prompted Home Guard commanders to order church bells to peal across the country to rally its members. This fully alerted the public. The following day, with no sign of any invasion imminent, General Headquarters had to stamp out the panic which they had inadvertently begun. The Home Guard was henceforth firmly instructed that on no account were church bells to be run by any member unless he had personally seen twenty-five parachutists land.[4]

Spy-catching was serious business. Evacuee Alan, upon being initiated into the local gang in Stoney Common village, was set the testing task of 'following suspicious men who could well be German spies and reporting back to our leader'. In Leeds, West Yorkshire, Ernest and his friends spent many nights lying in a field spy-watching. Across the road was a shop with the name of Schmiddy and the boys were convinced that with a name like that the shopkeeper must be German and therefore it stood to reason that he was a bona fide enemy agent. The boys maintained a nightly vigil after rumours had been heard that a light had been seen flashing from the shop during an air raid. During the day they would frequently go into the shop and throw suspicious side-ways looks at the baffled shopkeeper: 'We would all be looking at him – Schmiddy, a German.'

With thousands of people relocating all over Britain, the surge of strangers into established communities meant that the enemy could be on the doorstep. After a particularly close air raid, little Jill's mother, 'being very protective of her brood', adamantly refused to come out of her Anderson when she heard a man's voice because she was 'quite convinced it was an English-speaking [German] parachutist'. It was in fact the local ARP man. For those people who had relocated it was not easy to find their way about in a new place, particularly when all the signposts had been removed for security reasons, but being unsure of one's bearings could easily be interpreted as highly suspicious behaviour. When Vincent walked home from school one day he was 'stopped by a man who asked the way to Hill Top . . . the propaganda machine had already got through to an impressionable lad like me and I was fully aware of the need to "Be Like Dad, Keep Mum" and that "Careless talk costs lives". So, on the assumption that this stranger was probably a German spy, I directed him in the opposite direction from Hill Top and continued on my way home.' Vincent, feeling chuffed at having played a necessary part in the war, would later often wonder 'who the unfortunate man really was and whether he ever found his way to wherever he was going'. Derrick's father stopped to pick up a hitchhiker in his car but quickly got suspicious: 'He was sure the man was a spy because he didn't know the general direction of London.'

It was not always easy being the new arrivals in town during a period of heightened suspicion, and this could be used against people who did not fit in with their neighbours. Londoner Terry was evacuated with his family to Reading in Berkshire and felt that the locals there were quite hostile, especially when his father was unfairly accused of being an enemy agent. The ensuing hostility and brewing neighbours' dispute resulted in having a policeman at the door and 'plain-clothes men . . . sifting through all the household effects'. Terry thought that irate neighbours might have instigated this as they did not like the irregularity of his father's working hours, caused by ill health, nor his liking for practising the violin at home. In the market town of Otley, West Yorkshire, the arrival of a family who were considered to be 'foreigners' as they came 'from Leeds twelve miles away', made the locals uneasy. Julia, the daughter of the family, could not help but wonder 'if it was because of my father's moustache which may have reminded people of Hitler'. Such things roused suspicions and their activities began to be questioned: '. . . "they post a lot of letters," people said (mainly because 'they' were involved in organizing education of the Forces), and people recalled that the "help" was told not to go "in there" and disturb my father's papers (he was actually marking exams)'. Julia's father was reported for signalling the Germans during a raid after he was seen acting suspiciously with a torch one night. He was in fact in his garden showing his children a hedgehog.

An anxious man in Essex was thought to be a spy. The house next door to Basil's was up for rent and his parents had the job of showing potential viewers around: 'One day a middle-aged man carrying a small case called asking about the house. He then started asking questions about the bombing and guns etc.' While the man was viewing the house, Basil's family spied on him from behind the curtains of their windows. The stranger's activity looked very suspicious as they 'saw him standing in the bay window with the lid of his case upright and just staring out towards the Thames'. Fully alerted, the family reported the matter to the police. 'Some hours later the police came back, thanked them, and said that they had picked the man up. He was just a very nervous person with his lunch in his case.' Basil was really disappointed. Teenage Peter in Kent had a neighbour who actually could have been a spy: 'A spy was caught in Deal. He was in a teashop when he started to ask a lot of questions. A Marine thought he wanted to know too much so he called the Military Police who took him away to question him.'[5] The man, who was disabled and in a wheelchair, was not British but he and his wife were well-known to the locals and Peter and his pals would often play in their garden. After their arrest it was rumoured the couple had been sending wireless signals to the enemy from a transmitter concealed in the wheelchair.

A family of spies were caught in East Finchley. Nine-year-old Derek's new Austrian neighbours appeared friendly at first, in fact so much so that they declared to Derek's parents: 'We have taken a liking to your charming children, so when Hitler arrives you need not worry about them as we will look after them and see that they are safe.' Though this announcement did not raise alarm bells at the time, events soon turned sinister. Someone on Derek's street was emitting radio signals during air raids. The local police set up 'a radio transmitter detector based at the Police Station in the Archway Road on the old A1 . . . but one detector alone could not accurately pinpoint the source of the transmission. It was eventually agreed that a second detector would be set up on the flat roof at my father's office block at Crouch End, Hornsey.' It was a worrying time for Derek as the coordinates of the signals appeared to cross directly over his house, earmarking his family as possible spies. The signals were eventually found to be coming from a wireless concealed in a refrigerator in the house of the Austrian family. Derek and his mother, peering from behind the curtains of the front bedroom window, watched as the police escorted the neighbours from their house and took them away. They never saw or heard from them again.

People had to be very careful who they employed. The new maid from Germany in John's house, who unfortunately showed 'an admiration for Hitler' and a 'deep interest in Croydon Airport', disappeared all of a sudden. Jennifer's new governess also behaved 'very oddly'. She was heard 'typing in her bedroom at night' and was found 'burning papers in the boiler'. Even more suspicious, she had been seen in possession of a camera, walking towards the nearby RAF tower and visiting a house 'where lights had been seen at night – a fearful transgression'. The governess was reported to MI5 and was promptly fired. She stayed living locally but Jennifer and her friends kept up their wartime vigilance: 'My friends and I used to spy on her from behind the hedge. She had stuck the Victory logo, three dots and a dash, on her window. This represented the Victory signal sent out by the BBC to Europe, based on the opening notes of Beethoven's Fifth Symphony. We were quite sure she was using this as a cover for her illicit activities as a spy.' Before too long, the governess disappeared.

The rumour amongst us kids was that all Germans had square heads!

Donald Williams

The closest most children on the Home Front came to witnessing the enemy on the ground was seeing German and Italian prisoners of war. Brian went on a sightseeing trip in Liverpool to view the German POWs clearing the rubble from bomb-damaged buildings. Having been brought up on wartime propaganda, his imagination had envisioned the enemy as 'creatures resembling the "Squander-Bug" festooned with small swastikas'. To his great disappointment, 'they looked just like us'.

For some youngsters, the sight of German POWs inflamed their patriotism. Brian in Southampton, now a young teen and having left school, regularly took the works bus to Vickers Supermarine in Hursley. When the bus passed the German POWs putting up their US Army-issue tents in a newly-erected barbed-wire compound, he and his work friends would shake their fists at the enemy and give V for Victory signs. But not everybody felt angry towards enemy prisoners. Betty liked to take home-made biscuits to the friendly teenage Germans interred at Alvaston Recreation Ground in Derby. She felt compassionate towards them and thought that some of them looked young and helpless, and a few seemed to be 'shell-shocked or broken in spirit . . . they had sad eyes'. Julia saw the POWs living in tents on marshy ground behind the high wire fence at a camp in Weston Lane, Otley, and she thought they all looked sad too. When German POWs were first billeted on Wanstead Flats, the local children including Jean could hardly wait to rush over to stare at these frightening enemy prisoners. On her first sight of the prisoners, Jean stopped in her tracks. They were not what she expected at all; in fact they looked hardly any older than her. She felt sorry for going.

Some POWs were busy breaking out of camps. Two of the biggest incidents involved ninety-seven determined Italians absconding from a camp in West Scotland in 1944,[6] and in 1945 seventy German prisoners tunnelled unseen out of their compound in South Wales.[7] Many prisoners were allowed out of camps to work as labourers. In Thames Ditton a German POW camp was situated on Claygate Lane, but it was the labour from the immediate post-war Good Conduct POW camp, built on the site of bombed houses in Greenwood Road, that benefitted the local community. The Sergeant-Major in charge of the camp was not averse to palming a packet of cigarettes in return for some free foreign labour. The wonderful décor and painting in Daphne family's living room (courtesy of two artistic Italians) was much admired, as was the beautiful mosaic the Italians created in front of the camp using bombing wreckage. Later, German POWs at the camp worked on the family's garden and made the children a swing from an ammunition box. Not all POWS laboured willingly. Disgruntled

Germans from Otley POW camp were not happy to be handed shovels and dispatched on a train to snowbound North Yorkshire to clear the Settle and Carlisle railway line. In protest, more than half of them 'lost' their shovels out of the train windows on the journey. They were forced to work in shifts under the threat of no hot cocoa, and in future the shovels rode in the guard's van.

Working outside of camps was not only a welcome break from camp life but gave POWs the opportunity for contact with the public. On a small farm in Scotland one family hired POWs as farm hands from a nearby camp and they taught their daughter to be open-minded about the enemy: 'Mother had a German friend in years gone by, the wife of a colleague at the Institute and a devout Quaker, so she always reminded us children that there were good as well as bad Germans.' A line was drawn though: no 'fratting' was allowed. Non-fraternization with the enemy was generally considered to be the politically and socially correct form. Irene worked as a messenger girl at the Tower Creameries factory which employed Italian POWs on the Slovat platform. She had to be careful not to give the POWs any attention 'for that would have been against the rules, not of the factory owners, but the other workers'.[8] Yvonne was allowed to fraternize, or did so anyway regardless, as she had discovered that not only were the German POWs friendly but they were an unexpected source of income: 'Some did beautiful work: bracelets done with the new plastic wire; very lovely they were. I became a business agent selling these at around 2/- each. I got £2 for one man, a princely sum at the time!'

John knew of POWs in Lee Valley who were employed as workers in the glasshouses. He noticed that 'the absolute hatred which was felt for Germans in general did not seem to be shown on a personal basis'. It was likely to be this attitude of not holding prisoners personally responsible for the war that enabled mutual friendships to blossom between prisoners and locals. Joan in Cambridgeshire had German and Italian POWs working on her family's farm and strong bonds were formed. One Italian POW lived in her house during the war, and after the war one of their German workers invited them to Germany for a holiday to say thank you to Joan's mother to whom he felt he owed his life: 'He always said my mother saved his life by taking care of him.' Olive had no fear of the Italian POWs that roamed around her village in Nottingham, and the only German prisoner in the village did the milk round and was fully accepted by the community. He later married and remained living in Nottinghamshire. Marriages between local girls and POWs after the war were not unusual. A German prisoner from Alvaston camp married a local girl and became a school teacher in Derby, and Corporal Gunter Reichel married a girl from a grocery shop in 1948 whilst still in residence at Selby POW Camp, North Yorkshire.

Chapter 5

Shortages

Our mother must have been a miracle worker with the food we had . . .

William Corry

Clandestine operations took place on a street in Ealing. On a cold February afternoon young Dorinda was sent on a secret butter mission 'with a carrier bag to a neighbour's house that I hardly knew. When I was taken into the front room, there on the table was a large block of butter being dissected and patted into small, half-pound portions and carefully wrapped. One or two packets were put into my carrier bag and I was sent back home with strong instructions not to tell anyone, and although a chatty child, I never did!'

Rationing was introduced in January 1940 as a precaution to ensure that Britain could survive a siege during the war years that lay ahead. In Olive's house, that meant furtively filling the zinc bath in the cellar full of tinned food: 'Government said no hoarding, but!!' The foods selected for rationing had to be those which had a guaranteed supply. Throughout the war the amounts allocated fluctuated and so did the items as different foods were added to the rationing list. Ration books were filled with food coupons which entitled people to set amounts of rationed items at the shops they had registered with. Jill thought rationing was not entirely fair. Having to register with one grocer for your vegetables and one butcher for your meat, rather than being able to shop around, meant 'the shopkeepers had you over a barrel'. She found it impossible to get black-market goods because 'if you were a "comer-in" (i.e. not a local born and bred) you were never favoured with any extras or "under-the-counter" food that were rumoured to exist'. However, the under-the-counter items and the black market were not just rumours; it very much depended on who you knew and how much money you had.

In Birmingham, sitting on a pantry shelf in Clive's house, was a golden-coloured tin referred to as the 'pot of gold'. This was Clive's family fortune: '. . . black-market sugar, which of course was "gold"'. Teenage Gillian in Surrey knew very well that 'the black market thrived, enabling people to buy rationed goods at an inflated price and men known as "Spivs" operated this type of venture', and Brian discovered that his wealthy uncle 'always seemed to get odd things on the black market, for he visited pubs and had plenty of money'. Evacuee Jo was not even aware of rationing as her foster parents in South Wales 'appeared to have pots of money' and had plenty of food, and the two were not unconnected. Jo was 'warned never to talk about what we ate, or how much butter we had'. Philip in Gloucestershire was the same age as Gillian but he was not aware of any black-market items for sale; that might have had something to do with having a policeman for a father.

I was sent by my mother to get some pigs trotters from the butcher . . . and he said he had none as they had all run away because of the air raid.

William Corry

In Coventry, people heading to the butchers either carried newspapers to wrap their meat in or they took a dinner plate with them. Little Mary Lou's family in Bournemouth did not get any extras from their butcher who appeared to be struggling to even provide beef. The problem with the beef supply, he informed Mary Lou's mother as he leaned in close over the counter, was that he had 'to cut out huge pieces of diseased meat from some TB infected carcasses he had received'. While the Bournemouth butcher was dealing with contaminated corpses, a clergyman was driving around Nottingham with a boot-full of contraband. He had the body of a pig concealed in his car. When he was stopped by a policeman who asked what he had in the boot, the vicar replied, 'Half a pig'. 'The policeman thought he was joking and didn't look.'

New meats started to be seen in butcher shops. Felicity, waiting in a long queue outside the butchers in Hereford Street, Sheffield, saw for the first time horse and whale meat for sale. Irene in London tried whale meat and knew that 'some people tried horsemeat, but it was not popular'. Colin, also in London, did attempt eating horsemeat but his family preferred to feed it to the cat. His mother 'would go into Croydon to the horsemeat butcher and queue for meat', pretending it was her family as 'horsemeat was for human consumption only, not for animals, but most of the people were buying for their animals'. In Romford, people queuing in continental butchers nodded approvingly at the slabs of horse steak on display, saying 'how nice' horsemeat was (and no doubt their pets agreed), but Basil's family, British to the core, 'could never bring themselves to try it'. Another new meat appeared on the shop shelves from America: SPAM, a luncheon meat made of chopped pork shoulder and ham. Irene discovered it was 'fairly palatable when coated with batter and fried' and ate it for supper. Visitors to Olive's house might find themselves offered a nice SPAM sandwich or a finger-buffet of hot SPAM chunks fried in batter, while in one London restaurant Jambon de Valenciennes au Choux (hot SPAM) and Jambon de Strasbourg aux Endives (cold SPAM) was served with a flourish to the tables of the upper classes.[1]

Game was not rationed and rabbit was often served at the table. Gordon regularly ate rabbit and was usually given the task of going to the market at the end of the day with a sixpence to buy a rabbit for Sunday lunch. Terry in London would not eat rabbit on any account so his mother resorted to secretly skinning and cooking rabbit with the theory that once beheaded and cooked no-one could tell rabbit from chicken. Terry was not fooled. Even he knew that chickens did not have four legs. Mary Lou would watch the post, waiting for dinner to arrive – a pheasant which was delivered 'with just an address label around its neck'. Philip's father sourced his own. He had 'two 12-bore shotguns and also a recently acquired a 0.22 sporting rifle' and when the war started he 'quickly took himself off to his favourite gun shop in Gloucester and bought a goodly supply of shotgun cartridges and 0.22 ammunition'. With these he was able to provide rabbit, hare, partridge and also the occasional pheasant, all 'liberated' from the Duke of Beaufort's estate: 'Our mouths are as good as theirs,' justified Philip's mother as she plucked another Beaufort partridge. Pigeon was also on the menu at Philip's house, though in his mother's opinion 'the only part of a pigeon that was any good was the breast', but they made for a 'fine casserole'. There was however one culinary boundary which Philip's family would not cross: 'Some folk ate rooks. We definitely did not. We drew the line at rooks.'

Fish was also not rationed, but supplies could not be guaranteed as the Government had requisitioned around 75 per cent of fishing trawlers for the war. The smaller and less proficient trawlers that remained faced seas teaming with marauding U-boats and sea mines, resulting in the deaths of over 1,000 British fishermen. With fish and chips being off-ration, John in Waltham Cross could 'buy a penn'orth of chips but later two penn'oth (less than 1p) became the minimum'. Paper was scarce so people had to provide their own newspaper for wrapping their fish and chips: '. . . if you saw someone going along the road with a newspaper they were probably heading for the chip shop'. John, eating his chippie dinner back at home, often found he could read his chips 'if the ink was a bit fresh'. Ernest's mother liked fish, especially free fish, and she provided many a good dinner by bringing home sardines and 'a bit of whitebait' in her pinny from her job in the fish cannery in Hunslet, Leeds.

> *. . . The National Loaf was awful, of a rather dull colour between grey and brown and not particularly tasty.*
>
> *Philip Clutterbuck*

Bread was never rationed during the war, but in 1942 white flour was replaced by National Wheatmeal Four. This had a higher extraction rate than white flour, meaning that the mills could produce more flour from grain. It did not prove popular. Vincent's grandmother was not prepared to put up with anything but clean white flour and so spent much time illegally sieving National Flour through one of her stockings. White sliced bread disappeared from the shops to be replaced by the National Loaf made from National Flour. For the sake of economy a loaf was now smaller, unwrapped, unsliced and was not allowed to be sold until it was a day old. One fifteen-year-old boy in Coventry found the colour of it off-putting as it was 'an off-white greyish colour' and the taste even less appealing as it 'didn't taste like "proper" bread', but 'you got used to it'. In his Gloucestershire village, Philip missed his crusts: 'The National Loaf was awful . . . it never had a really nice crust.' Not surprisingly, the loaf earned the nickname Hitler's Secret Weapon.

A shortage of chicken feed led to a shortage of chickens, which in turn led to a shortage of eggs. Jill got in a predicament when 'a girl from school insisted on inviting me home to tea, without asking her mother first. I knew it would probably cause a problem but she was persistent. The expression on her mother's face, as she cut a poached egg in two for us, spoke volumes. Of course my mother asked the girl back the following week and we shared our rations with her. One had to be so careful not to rock the boat.' The ration allowance allowed just one egg per week, two if you were vegetarian, and unless you kept your own hens there was no substitute until powdered egg appeared from America. Mary Lou had scrambled eggs made from 'a yellow dried egg powder . . . mixed with either milk or water' but thought it tasted 'like India rubber, and became like it when trying to fry the mixture'. In a small mining village in Durham, disappointingly flat Yorkshire puddings were served with 'murmured apologies' at the Sunday dinner table. Vincent's grandmother, as if she did not have enough culinary conundrums to cope with considering the flour situation, was most peeved that she could not get her Yorkshire puddings to rise with these 'new-fangled dried eggs'. In Usk, Christine's father, a parish priest, had his contacts when it came to black-market eggs. It was one of his parishioners who acted as his supplier, 'an action which would have been frowned on if known about'. Clive in Birmingham was one of many who decided to 'give up our egg quota and grow chickens instead'. He started his new venture by swopping his dad's jumper for his first chicken.

> *. . . The day that a boy brought a fresh banana to school and deposited the skin in the waste bin. Half the school queued up to look at it . . .*
>
> *Brian Ferris*

The one fruit that was missed most during the war was the banana. In fact, some children like Maureen had never even seen a banana. It was not until the end of the war, when Maureen was about ten, that she saw her very first banana and it was a day she would always remember: 'Gran's greengrocery merchant brought the first banana into Dudley Wood. It was tiny and green and she hung it on a piece of string in the shop window for everybody to see. One little girl said to me that it was cruel to show it when people couldn't have one to eat, but I was so proud and thought it was wonderful – AND I GOT TO SMELL IT! It was the most wonderful smell after five years of waiting.' In Basil's house his mother concocted 'mock banana sandwiches' made by 'boiling and mashing up some parsnips and adding banana essence'. The result was so convincing that Basil's aunt politely refused a second serving as it would be 'depriving the children of them'.

Christine never saw a banana until after the war and had 'to be shown how to eat them'. For East-Ender Charles it was not the eating but the ripening that foxed him. He had hidden his first ever banana 'in a bedroom cupboard until its metamorphosis was almost complete'. When his banana was thoroughly black and well-rotted, he attempted to eat it and was really 'disappointed by its taste and mushy texture'. For John in Waltham Cross, it was not the banana but the grapefruit that captured his imagination after he saw a picture of one in a school book. It became his 'ambition for years to have one'. He waited the entire war for that lovely grapefruit only to find it was 'one of the biggest disappointments of my life when I peeled it and ate it like an orange and found it to be bitter'.

Tinned fruit was available in limited quantities. Vincent's grandmother saved 'one or two treats such as tinned pineapple chunks' for a rainy day, and these 'survived the entire war at the back of the pantry shelf waiting for the rainy day to arrive'. For Irene, 'tinned fruit was a dream',[2] and for Fred's sister Betty it was classed as one of the family's 'treasured possessions', a view not shared by her father when he discovered that the heavy suitcase, which he had just lugged back and forth across the Scottish moors at night during an air raid, was not full of important family items but 'a dozen or so cans of fruit saved from pre-war years'. R.J. spent many an air raid staring up at the ceiling of his fortified dining room, willing for that special emergency situation where he would be allowed to get at the hoarded tins of Melon & Ginger jam that had been hidden up there. It was possible to buy jam in the war, but somehow it did not seem to taste quite the same anymore. The ingredients were somewhat suspect. Olive's suspicions about shop-bought jam were confirmed when she was told by a Norfolk farmer that 'they supplied the local jam factory with swedes or mangolds so shop jam was just flavoured compote'. Jam rumours spread. Julia heard that 'because of such national economising . . . jam was made from sugar and root vegetables'. Not only that, but in addition this fake jam was made 'with wooden "pips" added for authenticity'.

The Government campaigned vigorously for people to grow their own vegetables to replace imports and save shipping. Muriel's father, like so many others all across Britain, grew his own food in the 'Dig for Victory' campaign. Back gardens, sports fields, parks and any available patch of ground were dug up and cultivated. A Hampshire hotel filled in its outdoor swimming pool and used it to plant potatoes. John's father in South Wimbledon had an allotment on the playing fields, and eight-year-old Ernest in Leeds helped dig up the school rugby pitch to plant potatoes, much to the sports teacher's dismay. In Coventry, the headmaster of the semi-demolished, war-torn King Henry VIII Grammar School gained a reputation for being 'notorious' in his war efforts, not just for using pupils as coke shovellers to keep the school boilers going but for conscripting green-fingered pupils for growing vegetables and tending his swine herd. The national vegetable campaign was such a success that in 1941 a 250-ton vegetable mountain quietly rotted away in a Government emergency reserve warehouse in Covent Garden.[3]

In Felicity's house, the simple carrot elevated to a must-have ingredient in many of her mother's recipes such as jams and cakes, a conviction encouraged nationwide by a Ministry of Food crusade designed to popularize the carrot as an alternative option for rationed food. It was also a handy way of getting rid of Britain's carrot surplus. An urban myth spread by the Government suggested that it was the carotene in carrots that benefitted the vision of Britain's night-fighter pilots. This helped to keep the real reason – radar – secret. Felicity heard that the carrot campaign caused some over-enthusiastic supporters to get carotoderma from eating too many carrots, 'they had an orange glow'.

When sweets began to get short before rationing I used to go around to the local greengrocer and buy a carrot to munch.
David Beedell

The versatile carrot also became the new sweet. On her way to school each morning Betty would call in at the greengrocer who 'would scrub clean his carrots and sell them at a halfpenny each. These were quite popular.' The ration system allowed everyone over five years old, including adults, their own weekly set of personal points for their 200 grams of sweets. It was not a lot. A Saturday trip to Woolworths for your sweets would see you take home maybe just seven sweets from most of their sweet range. Margaret in Otley could not help but notice the distinct scarcity of sweets; in fact they were 'virtually unobtainable' and children were often seen queuing outside the chemist where they could sometimes get 'Ovaltine tablets, liquorice root, etc'. Sweet-deprived Margaret and a friend once spent their pocket money in desperation on 'buying Rennies and something resembling hard black shiny coal, which must have been a kind of laxative, from the chemists. Apparently we were quite ill on this mixture!' She would never again be able to bear the taste of chalky peppermint.

Little Mary Lou in Bournemouth pushed her doll's pram up the road to get her sweet and chocolate supply from the French Canadians billeted there. Her favourite sweet was 'St. Ival lemonade crystals in a jar' eaten using sticky fingers. 'Our fingers turned bright yellow and I dread to think what the severely acid crystals did to our teeth.' There was always the option of making up your own sweets. Irene made up 'little mixtures of cocoa powder and sugar in a twist of paper for something sweet to eat',[4] and Clive's mother also turned her hand to confectionery, making her son's sweets 'concocted from old, dry Madeira cake, mixed with marmalade and cocoa, then made into little balls and rolled in sugar. "Chocolate Surprises" she used to call them'. In London, Henri's mother was inventive in providing her son with sweet snacks, making up 'a small mustard jar full of cocoa powder and sugar which I used to lick my finger and dip into under the desk during lesson time'. For Henri, nothing could quite equal shop-bought sweets. His favourites were 'aniseed balls and gob-stoppers . . . especially the really big ones that changed colour by layer as you sucked them'. Basil in Romford could get 'Mars, Milky Way and Kit Kat', and Derrick in Salisbury liked his 5p 'chocolate slam-bar or button-bar'.

What a pity that no medals were ever struck for mothers.
William Corry

Every morning after prayers, the evacuee girls from Sheffield's Notre Dame School sat down to a chilly breakfast in the neglected interior of Derwent Hall, Derbyshire. Breakfast was served on long tables which boasted 140 bowls of cornflakes pre-loaded with copious amounts of sugar. Because Charles lived in the heart of the bombing in London he was lucky if he got any breakfast at all: 'Depending on the previous night's damage to the home and its electricity, gas and water supplies, we had breakfast (or not) comprising mainly American Spam and dried egg prepared in so many different ways, or feeding

82

from the WVS and Salvation Army mobile canteens.' He could top up his mobile canteen breakfast with 'dinner in the government-sponsored local British Restaurant' for 'a "bob" (5p)'. These restaurants were staffed by volunteers, and by the beginning of 1942 there were 1,252 of these establishments in Britain.[5] Before the start of these Local Authority-run British Restaurants, dining out in restaurants was almost exclusively for the better-off who could afford to supplement their rations. The British Restaurants, which were started so 'that the less well-off could also benefit from having meals out', were more affordable for the average family. In Plymouth, teenager Desmond went to a school that did not provide dinner, so he had his in a British Restaurant which was 'a Nissen hut on a cleared bomb site', usually 'beans on toast which cost nine pence (4p)'. For Cleone in London, a fortnightly meal at a British Restaurant was something of a treat and left her with abiding memories of the 'smell of the mince and feel the condensation everywhere'. The town of Otley had a British Restaurant in a Nissen hut 'near the top of the bus station' where Julia's mother took her once, but they did not go again as 'Mother felt uncomfortable because she thought it was really meant for "the workers"'. Charles' grannie would absolutely not set foot in a 'posh' standard restaurant, proclaiming, 'I'd sooner have bread and dripping than "horses doovers" (hors d'oeuvres) that lot eat!' British Restaurants were more likely to be to her taste.

Rationing did not provide every family with the healthy diet it was intended to supply. In Scotland, rations did not work quite so well where one girl lived: 'They say we were healthier in wartime, but I doubt if that was true in the cold north of Scotland where there was a very poor variety of vegetables and certainly no fruit to speak of.' She felt that as a result of that 'we seemed to have a lot of time off with various infections, and to suffer a lot from boils'. Boils were not just common in Scotland as John found that they were prolific in Salisbury. These were usually treated with 'boracic ointment and pink lint dressing'. In addition, 'a patch of impetigo around the mouth would be cured by the application of a smear of vivid violet ointment (Gentian Violet)'. While impetigo was a common skin problem, it was the ever-increasing spread of scabies that most concerned the Ministry of Health. The number of scabies outbreaks in cities had soared during the immediate pre-war years and wartime conditions only made infection more likely. Known as a disease commonly spread in air-raid shelters, scabies earned the nickname 'Shelter Rash'.[6]

John in London considered that though they 'were generally very healthy youngsters', common childhood illnesses like 'scarlet fever, diphtheria, polio, tuberculosis, measles, chicken pox . . . could kill'. An outbreak of diphtheria in 1940 at a school for deaf and partially-deaf evacuees in Surrey was blamed on the amount of time all the pupils had spent crowded in their air-raid shelter: 102 of the children were hospitalized and four died.[7] At the end of the war it was noted that whereas around 8,000 children had been killed in air raids, nearly 9,000 had died from diphtheria.[8] Disease was a bigger killer than bombing.

On occasion, the old-time remedies for some ailments were not always the healthiest option. East End children who were suffering from 'whooping cough were taken for walks along the sewer bank (i.e. the Northern Outfall discharging East London's sewerage into the Thames) towards the Beckton Gasworks, so that they could breathe in the tar vapours from the factory'. The gasworks extracted gas from coal, and one of the by-products (coal-tar) was considered useful as an expectorant and disinfectant, therefore the pungent fumes from the gasworks were a source of free medication; providing you did not mind the ammonia and sulphuric acid that came with it. The children that Charles saw who were 'suffering from malnutrition' at his school in Canning Town were dosed with a large spoonful of cod liver oil and malt. 'For opening medicine [a laxative], long, hard and thick liquorice sticks were given to children to chew at endlessly and then told to lie on a horsehair pillow to "breathe in the smell".'

Taking 'opening medicine' was not nearly as embarrassing as the sun-ray treatment June had to endure at Uxbridge Hospital. At the tender age of fourteen she was forced to sit topless in group therapy with a group of elderly ladies sat around a sun lamp, this being a cure for early-onset 'rheumatism . . . caused by poison from infected tonsils'. In Paddington, a little boy also received sun-ray treatment. He had to have three sessions per week at St. Mary's Hospital in Pread Street, London, to cure his severe chilblains. His treatment package also included the dubiously-named 'electric baths'.

Rationing could not get rid of food poverty. People still needed money to feed their family and if they were poor then they could not always afford to buy their full allocation of rations. Baby Kathleen in Kent came from a very poor family and her abiding memory of growing up in the war years would be one of 'extreme hunger' and deprivation: '. . . as regards food I can mostly remember eating rabbits heads and pigs trotters and absolutely drooling over the thought of a boiled egg'. For some families, it was a never-ending battle on the kitchen front line to raise a family in the austerity of war. Jill's mother had 'to be tough, with a four-mile journey each way, in addition to queuing up in the shops and carrying a week's shopping. I think she was suffering for malnutrition too, as I am sure she gave most of her rations to Father and me. Her health was never robust and she fainted a lot.' In Gordon's house in West Yorkshire, 'in spite of all the help from kind relatives, friends and neighbours' their 'financial situation was dire'. His widowed mother could rarely afford to put meat on the table for her sons, and when she could it was only rabbit and occasionally sausage. Shirley's mother struggled to live on her husband's soldier's pay of 'thirty-six shillings (£1.80) a week'. Out of this she had to pay rent of ten shillings and 'consequently we were quite hard up'. Frequently, Shirley and her mother would empty all the purses in the house trying to cobble together enough money for a loaf of bread, and they often resorted to boiling the kettle on the fire because there was no penny for the gas meter. William's mother in Birkenhead found it a strain to feed her husband and two children: 'I do remember my sister and I, who were rebelling against the barley broth, had our heads dipped in the plate. Mother cried as she wiped our soupy faces. She would tell us that she would eat with Dad and then when he came home she said to him that she had eaten with us.'

CHILDREN IN THE SECOND WORLD WAR

*Patches on trousers. I dodged school one day because I had
more patches on my trousers than trousers.*

P. J. Cotton

Clothes rationing began in the summer of 1941 with sixty-six points
allocated per person per year, though this dropped as low as forty
points some years. Children could receive an extra ten points on top
of that if they met certain criteria. 'If your child was above average
height or weight you got extra coupons', a rule which Jane's
stepmother took full advantage of when it was time to apply for those
coveted extra coupons. She would strategically give the children a
heavy, stodgy meal before taking them by car (no walking off all that
food) to the chemists 'so that we wouldn't lose any weight on the way
and hope we were heavy enough'.

In Sheffield, Janet's school had 'the responsibility to weigh and
measure us regularly as well as check us for verrucae'. Janet received
extra coupons for needing 'shoes size six or over' which she found
'interesting' as her feet were never be bigger than size 5½ as an adult.
Those extra coupons proved useful though as there were eight people
in her family which necessitated a lot of careful juggling with clothes
coupons. Her older sister learnt to repair and resole shoes using their
father's 'hobbing foot, a cobbler's knife, wax and shoe leather', and
the youngest daughter wore 'clogs made in Rochdale' which were off-
ration. Gordon in West Yorkshire also wore clogs, black clogs, as it
was hard for his single-parent mother to afford shoes for three growing
boys who constantly wore them out. Gordon's mother promised her
boys that if it was at all possible they each 'might have a pair of shoes
each on our fourteenth birthdays'. The boys learnt to repair their clogs
'by re-soling them from discarded motorcar tyres'. Shod in clogs
which were hardly the height of fashion, the boys' plight did not go
unnoticed by a kindly Salvation Army Bandmaster who bought 'his
own son a pair of clogs to wear with his army uniform so that we
would not be embarrassed'.

The holes in the soles of Betty's shoes were patched with cardboard
and newspaper. She did occasionally get new shoes which always

arrived at night, procured by a 'furtive deal' on the black market, when 'a chap would call around with several pairs of children's shoes; we would try them on and presto had new shoes which gave us absolute bliss'. Jane and her friends at boarding school had the 'the toes cut out of our sandals and house shoes when they grew too short for us'. Her school started a 'second-hand uniform cupboard . . . and some mufti [ordinary] clothing was out in it as well, though mostly for the boarders'.

School uniforms were hard to budget for. Mary Lou's mother made all of her daughter's school uniform and blazers by hand, cutting up old clothes to make them and knitting 'grey school socks which were in Shetland wool and itched like mad'. Janet had no gym shoes as there was not any rubber available; that meant no elastic in her knickers either so 'we had buttons'. Six-year-old Shirley knew why the headteacher at her school was often seen changing a child's jumper in class. The Head bought new jumpers for those who were wearing worn-out clothes, though it was sometimes embarrassing for the children who received the headteacher's hand-outs as 'we were all aware of it and why it was done'. When Shirley moved up to senior school, 'the school provided means by which parents could buy second-hand uniform to help out with clothing coupons'. Shirley's 'white blouses were ex W.R.N.S from Millets, the Army and Navy stores, and one my mother made out of a pillow case'. Basil's clothing coupons somehow had to stretch to finding all the uniform required at his grammar school in Romford: '. . . school uniform, blazer, tie, socks, cap' and a 'gym and football kit'. It helped to take a trip to Romford market where people could bump up their clothing coupons by paying a 'fixed price per coupon . . . to make up the shortage', even though this was illegal. The stallholders kept an eye out for market officials or policemen during these covert transactions.

When Janet won a scholarship to Sheffield High School she had to have a dark brown uniform so all her family had to donate their own clothing coupons for her. As well as the basic uniform she needed 'a gym tunic and blazer, blouses, indoor shoes, outdoor shoes, brown knickers etc'. Her school coat was tailored out of an old blanket that had been dyed. Jill's parents also had to give up coupons to provide their daughter with uniform for St. Mary's School in Romford 'as private schools like convents didn't make allowances for rationing when it came to their uniforms'. Unfortunately her family then had to evacuate to escape the bombing and found themselves having to buy a whole new set of uniform once again for the new convent school, so 'more precious coupons' had to be forfeited. Jill could not help but think that 'people who had not experienced the Blitz had different priorities and little understanding'.

Charles and his friends in Canning Town attended 'the local Mission Church of St. Alban's in Butchers Road'. Their motivation had less to do with religious aspirations and more to do with the lure of the Bundles for Britain clothes parcels from America and Canada that were sent to the Mission. A lot of children like Charles had 'a minimum of clothing with a clean change just once a week'. He did not need a wardrobe as he had nothing to put in it; instead, his 'hanging rail was two odd sized nails banged into the back of the bedroom door'. The Bundles for Britain that arrived at the Mission contained donated clothes, boots and shoes, the footwear being separated into piles of left and right 'presumably to dissuade theft'. When Charles and his pals gratefully received their donated clothes they strutted out of the Mission sporting 'heavy-weight tartan-check lumberjack coats with deep fur collars and wearing thick check cowboy shirts', more suitable for Alaskan winters than the English summer. Charles' mother also went to the Mission for 'the Monday afternoon jumble sale which was supplied from the West End's rich people's throw-outs. The "price" was obligatory church attendance every weekday morning at 8.15am, on-route to school'.

Mum told me to sit on the path holding my bag of coal and not let anyone take it until she came back again. Those winters were cold.

Irene Elce

The winters in the 1940s were long and bitter. Because of the shortages of war everyone was encouraged to conserve fuel and services which meant limiting use of electric and heating at a time when families in poorly-insulated homes needed it most. During winter the heating was rationed in Irene's house in London: 'The electricity was turned off during much of the day and coal was also rationed.' Seven-year-old Irene's mother would walk with her daughter to collect a precious 'extra ration of coal. Each person was allowed one bag of approximately twenty-five kilos of coal briquettes'. The walk home carrying and dragging their heavy sacks of coal was a feat of endurance for both of them. With the 'extremely hard winters' and 'no coal to be had' one mother in London was desperate. She was forced to keep her children off school one day to take the long trip to the gas works where she could buy 'sixpennyworth' of coal in a cash-and-carry scheme. They used the baby's big pram to carry their sacks home.[9]

Coal was the only means of heating the house, and for those with a coal-fired range rather than a modern gas oven it was the only way of cooking. In Romford at Basil's house it could sometimes take forever to make a meal as 'there were voltage and as pressure drops during peak hours which made the lights even dimmer and the time taken to cook a meal longer as you patiently waited for the oven to heat up or the saucepan to boil'. With very little heating and no double glazing, buildings were almost as cold inside as outside. John had to sit in his coat during lessons at Kings Road School in Waltham Cross. Despite the fact his school had coal-fired central heating it was not always on as their 'coal used to run out because it was in short supply, and on those days we wore our overcoats in class and every so often we did ten minutes of exercises like marching on the spot or arm swinging'. For Irene, even the nights spent in the London Underground, 'where we were warm, even if we could not sleep well', were preferable to staying in their freezing-cold house.

In Nottingham, 'coal hammers and coal shovels were very important items in every home' because the coal sometimes arrived in great lumps and had to be smashed up to fit into the hearth. Coal was so precious in Nottingham that it was 'the only thing that needed to be locked up'. Janet's family was 'reduced to living in the kitchen except in the very warm weather as that was the only room with a fire'. To keep warm in bed at night she had a hot water bottle but when this eventually fell apart there were no replacements due to a shortage of rubber. Instead, a brick was warmed in the oven and wrapped in newspaper to make a bed warmer. In Liverpool, industrious young Charles was keeping the fire at home burning by reclaiming wood from bombed-out buildings; at least there was plenty of it.

Even children's bath time was affected by shortages as a regulation of no more than five inches of water in the bath was encouraged in order to save water. At Terry's billet in Island House evacuee hostel, water was conserved by having only 'one water change for every five children' during the regular Saturday bath night. In contrast, Brian in his billet with a wealthy family got a bath 'every night, three children in the same water, but one at a time, and in strict rotation so that each of us could be first'. Many homes, like one girl's billet in Herefordshire, did not have a bathroom. The cottage she was staying in not only had no bathroom but no water supply or electricity. Back at home it was not much better – whenever there was a little money to spare she could go to the 'public bathhouse but of course, my water had to be shared with my younger baby brother Fred and sister Eve'. The only other option was to 'light the gas oven in order to provide warmth for a strip wash in the scullery'.

In 1942 soap was rationed which added to the lack of kitchen and bathroom products. A mother in Coventry who had several children struggled to get enough soap to wash the never-ending mountain of nappies she needed. With her next baby due soon, she received a 'maternity bundle – a stout brown paper sheet for lying on for the delivery, and other bits and pieces for a home delivery'. Felicity found that wartime conditions meant she could 'not get hair grips or razor blades', and Philip's father, feeling the lack of the latter, resorted to 're-sharpening razor blades by rubbing them on the inside of a glass tumbler filled with water'. Janet discovered that the 'shortage of cotton caused a lack of sanitary towels, and unless you have experienced having to have reusable ones washed (cut up terry towelling nappies pinned to a piece of bandage around your middle), you cannot imagine how unpleasant that was'. Grace noticed that paper rationing meant that 'even the size of toilet paper decreased'. At least she had real toilet paper and a private toilet; many people had neither.

Gordon was living in his new house in Heckmondwike at the age of nine. The 'novelty of being able to have a bath in private with our own water and use an indoor toilet without the embarrassing expectation of someone wanting to join you' had taken a long time to wear off. Up until the age of seven he had to share a two-hole community toilet with neighbours and wash in a tin bath in front of the fire. The one habit his household maintained was not indulging in the luxury of toilet paper: '. . . we still had newspaper hung behind the door'. Little four-year-old Mick found the whole toilet experience a cause of confusion when he relocated to his grandfather's house in Rodley, Yorkshire, and it was not just because of the toilet paper. He sat in puzzlement the first time he visited Granddad's 'Singing Shed' which was located well away from the house down the garden, across the lane, in the vegetable patch. Inside the draughty shed, 'hanging behind the door on a big nail was a pile of old newspapers about six inches by eight inches in size'. There was no toilet in the shed, just a plank with a hole, and the door had a piece of string with a stick of wood tied to it. It took some explaining by Granddad to persuade Mick that this shed was indeed a toilet, a Yorkshire special: 'Noo look here lad, yon's a singing toilet, and yon sticks a grabber for when thee can't go or to keep door shut if it's windy.' There was an indoor toilet in Granddad's house but Mick was given strict instructions 'that it were for folk in't night-time or them as was sickly, not for thou to make a mess o' clartin' it up in't day!'

While it had been mentioned in the House of Commons that town boys evacuated to the country would be unable to cope with primitive rural toilets and would be bound to have certain health problems as a result, most MPs had probably not encountered urban community toilets.[10] Barker's Chip Shop, which Mick's other grandparents owned, stood in a cobbled street in Armley, Leeds, near the prison. At the top of the street squatted a row of communal water closets. The chip shop dutifully supplied the community toilets with toilet paper recycled from donated used newspapers. Sometimes the toilet paper was supplemented with 'Izal Toilet Tissues which were like wiping your bum on a sheet of greaseproof paper' or, if an unpopular family was known to frequent a particular toilet then that one was supplied with paper cut from the 'Illustrated News or the Post, which were shiny magazines . . . it could be quite funny to hear the swearing that went on when the "Morning Visit" had been made'. It was easy to tell if someone was on their way for a Morning Visit as they were usually carrying 'a length of string with a noose in it' as a substitute toilet flushing chain, the originals long since stolen. The wooden seats that once graced the communal toilets had also disappeared, to keep those home fires burning.

Chapter 6

Schools

Attendance at school for those of us who remained was reduced to two mornings a week of two hours' duration, which for those in my class evolved into one long chess lesson.

Charles Tyrrell

In Romford, Essex, eight-year-old Basil and his sister had decided not to evacuate, and that turned out to have an unexpected bonus. They had an extended holiday as their school, like many, remained closed. In London, the City Council stated that those schoolchildren not evacuated must not go to school until notice was given, a rule hard to break when there were not many schools left open. Just over 50 per cent of London's schoolchildren remained home, which represented a considerable number whose education was effectively terminated for the foreseeable future. By the end of the first week in September the problem of school closures in London was raised in the House of Commons. The concern was not for lack of education, but for the sheer numbers of children running wild on the streets.[1]

Many schools shut their doors because the majority of their pupils had evacuated with their teachers, leaving little or no alternative arrangements for those pupils who had opted out of evacuation. Brian in Southampton discovered his school had completely closed down as 'most of the teachers and pupils were evacuated to towns in the New Forest area. There were a few other boys who lived near me who also never went. So for the next six or seven weeks the school stayed closed.' In Leeds, teenage Ken found 'there were no schools open in the city because all the teachers had gone with the evacuees'. Also in

Yorkshire, Janet noticed that 'all the schools in Sheffield were closed from August 1939'. Another reason for school closures was the lack of air-raid shelter facilities in schools. While the Government's shelter policy had set off to a late start, part of the problem was that it had not expected to need schools, and therefore school shelters, in danger areas. The schoolchildren were supposed to have gone. Manchester had complied, with only 25 per cent of its children remaining in the city, but in some places like Bradford there was a reluctance to hurry: 75 per cent of Bradford's schoolchildren stayed home and had a holiday.[2]

The schools that did remain open, like Everton Terrace School in Liverpool where ten-year-old Charles went, faced disruption. Class sizes in this school had reduced: 'Numbers attending school had begun to diminish due to a trickle of children being sent away or evacuated for safety.' That was nothing compared to what would happen months later. With no evidence of war in sight as winter turned into spring, those who had been evacuated began to return, refilling classes once more and putting pressure on previously-closed schools to reopen. By January 1940 around one-third of the schoolchildren who had been evacuated from London moved back home. Due to this constant state of flux, schoolchildren returning during the 'Phoney War' found that it was not until April 1940 that it was compulsory to attend the hastily reorganized and reopened schools.[3] Education finally seemed to have some structure in place, the summer passed, and then the bombing started.

The start of the Blitz changed the whole scene once again, throwing education into a state of emergency. Another wave of schoolchild evacuation began. As the bombs pounded Liverpool, the trickle of pupils leaving Charles' school had become 'a flood'. His 'own class was soon reduced to no more than six pupils (which would eventually reduce to four) and all the other classes were in a similar state'. Charles noticed the reduction in teachers too 'as their ranks were reduced by call up or transferring to evacuation areas in the country to bolster the now-outnumbered rural schools' staff'. He found that his education was now condensed into a mere four hours per week where the curriculum consisted of board games.

A twelve-year-old girl helping to dig a trench for air raid protection in Kent, 1939. *(D. Rice)*

A 'homely' Anderson shelter. *(P. Tollworthy)*

A sketch of her family's Anderson by Christine Widger, aged twelve, drawn while sitting in the shelter during a doodlebug attack.

A brick surface shelter built at the bottom of a garden in Kingsmead Avenue, Tolworth, Surrey. *(E. Gardener)*

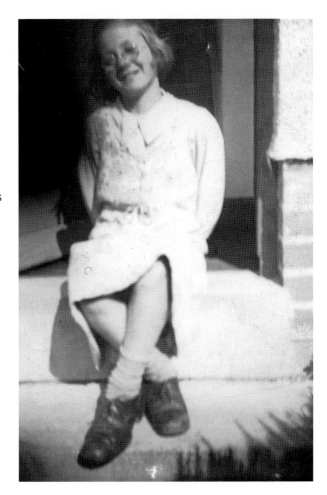

GOVERNMENT EVACUATION SCHEME: LIVERPOOL.

Code No. X 111/3   Party No. S 1

Name Hoyle Nesta

Home Address 45B Granby St

School

Evacuee's label. *(W. Hayle)*

Phyl Jones, privately evacuated from East London with her siblings for the duration of the war.

Muriel Booth, aged eleven, who was evacuated on a Thames paddle steamer.

Muriel Booth's plea to come home from evacuation.

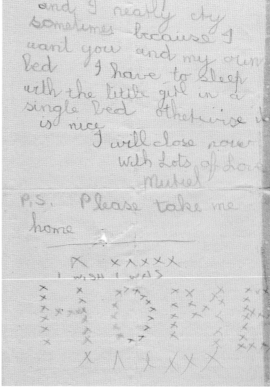

and I really cry sometimes because I want you and my own bed I have to sleep with the little girl in a single bed otherwise it is nice I will close now with lots of love Muriel

P.S. Please take me home

X X X X X X
I WISH I WAS

X X X X X X
X X X X X X X X
X X X X X X X X
X X X X X X

X X X X X

Kitty Levey (right) and her sister, CORB evacuees, ready to depart from Lancashire to South Africa.

Jo Veale from Birmingham who was convinced she was 'going home on Monday'. She did not return home for six years.

Christine Widger, evacuated from Kent to Lancashire, kept in touch with her Lancashire teacher for the next fifty-seven years.

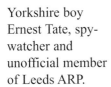

Yorkshire boy Ernest Tate, spy-watcher and unofficial member of Leeds ARP.

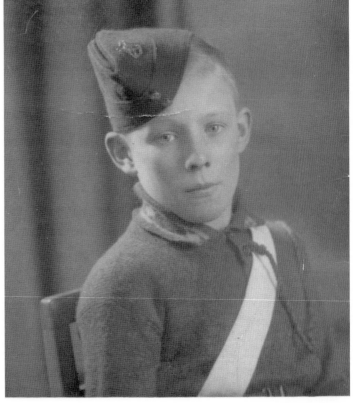

Daphne Hackett, aged eleven, whose family befriended prisoners from Thames Ditton POW Camp.

German prisoners at Thames Ditton POW Camp, Greenwood Road, Thames Ditton, Surrey. October 1946. *(I. Leggatt)*

Dorinda Simmonds of Ealing, London, black-market butter girl.

Derek Clark's school, semi-demolished overnight by a doodlebug in 1944.

A little boy in Kent playing with his father's ARP kit. *(M. Jones)*

Iain Leggatt playing war games, 1942.

Alan Starling (left), underage member of the 3rd Battalion Renfrewshire Home Guard, Scotland.

Geoff Creece, GPO messenger boy in Portishead during the Bristol Blitz.

John Bones in uniform as Flight Sergeant in No. 308 Squadron Air Training Corps, Colchester.

Joyce Garvey (1942), who helped a mother give birth in an air-raid shelter, member of Birmingham ARP from the age of sixteen.

Jean Wilson wearing her St John Ambulance cadet uniform.

Jean Wilson, member of Friern Barnet Girls Training Corps, London.

Myfanwy Khan with her older sisters in the garden of her home in Exeter.

The ruins of Myfanwy Khan's home after the Exeter Blitz, 1942.

Margaret Hofman, whose family fled the docklands of London during the Blitz.

Sketch of a doodlebug by Jeff Nicholls who was an industrial spotter in London for the Alarm within the Alert.

-the terrible silence following a flying bomb engine stopping.

John Pincham (left) and his brother at home in Wimbledon Park the year before they were bombed-out.

Bomb-damaged houses in John Pincham's street, 1944, which had to be guarded from looters.

VE Day street party in Rothsay Road, Gosport. *(M. Brien)*

SCHOOLS

Southampton was repeatedly targeted by the Luftwaffe and in 1940 Brian found that in his reopened school, rather than the situation getting better, 'things . . . now got worse'. Teachers were scarce in his school as so many had been conscripted for the Forces or transferred to other, more desperate schools, so classes were forced to share teachers and the curriculum quickly fell apart: 'Some days we went to school for half a day. On some half days we used to go for rambles in the woods near the school so in case of an air raid we were away from the school.' Nightly bombing meant lots of absences, and one day Brian turned up at school 'after a night with lots of alarms and there were only about twelve of us. There was no fuel, so we all stayed in the Headmaster's room by his fire with about three teachers. After a while he sent us home.'

Little five-year-old Ann in Croydon started at a school which was chronically short of teachers. She sat on a long wooden bench in a row of desks 'which held two pupils, all facing the front, with the desks in rows' in a class of up to fifty pupils. If a teacher was absent then that class had no choice but to squeeze three to a desk with the other classes. Four-year-old Sylvia also had a large class of fifty in her reception class but 'it didn't feel overcrowded, I didn't know any different'. Even during the bombing, schoolchildren were never static. There were frequent relocations and many children drifted home. When little Betty returned to South London in 1941 after her evacuation, she got the good news that Pollards Hill School was about to reopen as the majority of its pupils had returned from evacuation. The school was very overcrowded as it had taken in pupils from a nearby bomb-damaged school, so every desk was shared by three children. The benches were placed so close together the children had to 'scramble over some to get to those towards the back of the classroom'. Class numbers were high in Betty's school, 'with sixty to seventy children in a class', the most being seventy-two in one class. During the 1942 bombing of Bath, nine-year-old Michael had no school at all: 'My school, on the Bear Flat, had closed on the night of the Blitz, never to reopen, so I had nowhere to go immediately.' He had little choice to try his hardest to pass the entrance exam to another school and managed to get accepted, underage, to the City of Bath Boys School though it took him 'two or three years to get into my right "stream"'. For Michael and many other children, the disruptions caused by the unpredictability of war were taking their toll.

With the educational system disrupted, disbanded and on its knees barely six months in to the war, the MP for Aberavon berated the House of Commons with the words, '. . . if anybody has paid the price for this war up to now, it is the children more than any other section of the community'.[4] Education, and therefore schoolchildren, had become an unforeseen casualty of war.

. . . We travelled with two goats in our coach!

Denise Iredell

Those schools that were evacuated faced the task of keeping pupils and classes together and it proved to be far from straightforward. Some fee-paying grammar and private schools moved lock, stock and barrel to a specific residence. Thirteen-year-old Denise evacuated with Stonar House School, Kent, which relocated to a Wiltshire mansion with those pupils who were weekly boarders. Her school travelled in coaches along with a menagerie of 'various pet animals ranging from white mice to cats and dogs, birds, rabbits and horses', not forgetting the resident school goats which rode in the bus with the girls. In Sheffield, a convent school was also on the move. Twelve-year-old Audrey got ready to be evacuated with the school to Derwent Hall in Derbyshire: 'It must have been an absolute nightmare to organize, as everything had to be transported from Sheffield – chairs, tables, crockery, blackboards, piano, etc., but finally, in September 1940, one hundred and forty girls and eight teachers travelled to Derwent.' There was no hot water at first, and no heating ever, in the seventeenth-century building that became their new home and school. It was certainly a novel experience for both the staff and children, one which Audrey described as 'unique', but 'after one year the deprivations and stress on the teaching staff became too much, and the Board of Education declared that living conditions were intolerable'. The school returned to Sheffield, with the Head noting that 'older girls found life very hard' in Derwent Hall, 'but the younger girls fell in love with the life, were insensitive to drawbacks and gained much from the long walks, freer open-air life, and the space for adventure.' Audrey, one of the younger girls, absolutely agreed.

State schools had to billet their schoolchildren with whoever would take them. Some schools were able to keep their pupils close together in the same area, while others found their pupils billeted miles apart like Pat's grammar school which was 'spread out over twelve villages' in Worcestershire. Small rural schools and those which were already at maximum capacity faced the difficulty of accommodating an irregular influx of extra pupils throughout the war as schoolchildren arrived, left, and then another wave of evacuation due to bombing brought more pupils in again. The local village school in Nunney, Somerset, that one evacuee girl attended was 'overcrowded and education was very limited'. Her lessons were restricted to 'doing exercises from a book and handing it to the person in the next desk to be marked'. She would later feel that this was really detrimental to her learning and that her 'education never recovered from this period'. When one boy moved to where his father was stationed at Canons Pyon in Herefordshire, he discovered that the local village school had 'three classes all held in one large room with the three backboards side by side, one for each class. Sitting in one class you see and hear what's going on with the others.' He found it was 'very distracting to say the least'. Class sizes were large at the local school in Chertsey where another boy was billeted. His school was 'in a large hall with over 120 pupils' and just three teachers ('one each for the infants, juniors and seniors'). One teacher went on permanent sick leave, therefore the boy and his brother were put 'in a class of over eighty varying in age from eight to fourteen' and 'the poor teacher didn't stand a chance, but she never seemed stressed or irritable'.

Jill was not very happy when she had to attend a small primary school in Stapleford, Hertfordshire. Collected by 'an ancient taxi' that rounded up children from neighbouring villages, she was taken to a two-roomed school: '. . . a small one for the infants and a large one where the older children sat on one side and the younger ones on the other, while two teachers sat at a large table, one teaching the older class and one the younger.' It was difficult to follow the lessons as both teachers were 'often speaking at the same time' and Jill's teacher appeared distracted as she 'knitted incessantly'. One ten-year-old girl found herself far from home 'deep in the wilds of Northumberland' where the small village school had a similar set-up to Jill's. Her school 'comprised [of] two rooms, one for the tinies and the other for everyone else. If we were bored with our lesson, we simply turned our head and listened to the other.'

Despite the educational disadvantage that evacuation could bring, integrating children into different schools did have the social benefit of enabling children from diverse backgrounds to mix – though not always in a way in which teachers would approve. Ten-year-old Londoner Michael was the new boy and a 'Vac' as he was called ('in the jargon of the Burnley boys') at Wood Top School in Lancashire. According to an unofficial but traditional custom, Michael was expected to accept the challenge for school champion: '. . . this had nothing whatever to do with academic achievement but was based purely on who could beat the current incumbent in a fist fight, settled after school in a nearby field'. So momentous was the event that nearly the whole school turned up to watch as Michael fought and won the 'Cock of the Midden' title, after which he was firmly accepted into the hierarchy of the playground as leader and disciplinarian of all playground disputes. The newly-crowned Michael went on to lead the Wood Top School gang to victory in the after-school battle with the boys from Hargher Clough School, a sporting event which 'engendered team spirit and established a respected code of practice'.

Janet, temporarily at St James School in Royston on evacuation, did not particularly enjoy integrating into the small Lancashire school. A gang of boys known as the 'Gravel Hole Gang', clog-wearing schoolboys, were very intimidating. In the small town of Harpenden in Hertfordshire, it was the evacuees that formed a troublesome gang. The Crooning Gang (eight schoolboys from Enfield, London) were not integrating well into their new community. In January 1940 they were in court for a fourth time for ten counts of theft from local shops.[5] Integrating was even harder if you were fleeing from prejudice in another country. Refugees turned up unexpectedly in some schools, including St James' where Janet found the appearance of the two new boys 'strange' because 'they spoke no English and wore funny trousers with leather straps'. When she attended Sheffield High School 'two sisters arrived at the school . . . they were Jewish refugees from, I believe, Austria'. Janet was not really quite sure of why they were at her school, the explanation did not appear to be part of the curriculum, and it was only later in life that she understood the circumstances which led them to be there. Jane, aged eight, knew nothing about Judaism when three Jewish children from inner London arrived in her school: 'I knew nothing about the diaspora and thought Jews were people in the Bible who lived in Israel . . . I couldn't understand why they weren't allowed to take part in the Christmas Play.'

Seven-year-old John had come to London from Hungary a few years before the start of the war due to anti-Semitism. He felt distinctly out of place when he arrived at Addison Road School 'dressed in normal Budapest wear for little bourgeois boys – white sailor suit incorporating a big navy blue collar with white stripes, black bows tied below the neck and a cotton undershirt' complete with 'white kid leather boots with black patent leather toecaps'. He immediately came face to face with another form of prejudice: bullying. After running the gauntlet of the playground bullies on his first day, his mother sent him to school the next day 'dressed more like a good Cockney boy'.

One morning we arrived at school to be greeted by a great pile of rubble where our new classrooms and science block had stood.

John Tomes

For the children who remained at home in high-risk areas or returned there after a period of evacuation, apart from the uncertainty as to whether their school would be open there was no guarantee that their school building would still be standing. 'On a never-to-be-forgotten morning' Terry walked down Tottenhall road only to find it was 'choked with people, fire engines and police cars'. The school had 'been hit by a score of incendiary bombs, and the top floor was burnt out'. His school was shut until desks could be salvaged from the wreckage and moved into the hall of the Infants School next door. One thirteen-year-old had been accepted at King Henry VIII Grammar School, Coventry, but was shocked to find that the building was nearly derelict: 'Only the exterior walls were left standing' and 'the whole of the interior of this building had been destroyed by fire in the Blitz of April 1941'. Broken but undefeated, the school remained open. Assembly was held in the playground every morning, rain or shine, and lessons were held 'in the army-style huts built at the rear of the school alongside the playing field'. London boy Brian returned to West Acton Primary School in London after his evacuation. This school had 'been damaged by bombing, two classrooms out of action and boarded up, and coping stones blown off the roof of the hall'. His classroom was now in the staff room and 'the accommodation was very cramped'. It did not get any better when he moved to St Clement Danes Grammar School, Hammersmith, which was distinctly showing signs of the war. The 'centre part of the left wing of the building had been demolished in an air raid, so the school was cut in two'. In winter he sat huddled in his coat in a temporary classroom, the small stove in the corner barely making any effect on the chill in the air.

Michael was now at The City of Bath Boys' School which had been ravaged during the Bath Blitz 'by a frontal assault with cannon shells from low-flying aircraft and the two upstairs rooms (one a lecture theatre, one a laboratory) either side of the main entrance were burnt out and remained closed for a long time. Damage to the stonework was evident for some years after.' At least his school was still standing, unlike John's school in London which had been hit by a V1 in the night. He arrived at school the following morning 'to be greeted by a great pile of rubble where our new classrooms and science block had stood'. Barbara's school in Stroud Green was another building damaged by a V1, this time during school hours. 'The doodlebug had landed a little way up the street . . . so all the children had to be sent home again.' Barbara, whose mother was not at home that day, stayed on at school to help clean up. She was busy sweeping the glass out of the art room when it was quietly pointed out to her that hanging precariously above her head was the rest of the broken glass roof: 'A little jog would have sent it down on top of me.' Dulwich College was hit by a doodlebug in the night, destroying the armoury, demolishing half of the science block and damaging the swimming pool. It was a relief to pupil Derek to discover the school was closed. He had not finished his homework.

After Sheffield's first major blitz, Janet was pleased to find her primary school was closed but was a bit 'disappointed to discover it was quite undamaged'. Basil was another child disheartened to find his school still standing. Though the Infants School Hall had burned down after being hit by incendiary bombs, the Junior School Hall stood undamaged and his school resumed as normal. In Birkenhead, William's school was destroyed by a landmine, but what really bothered him was that buried in the wreckage was his precious new pencil, the one with his name printed in gold: 'I don't think I ever forgave the Germans for that act of destruction.'

For school children evacuees their new school could be something of a surprise. Denise's classroom in the grounds of Cottles Park was a greenhouse. It was freezing in winter with no heating at all and 'even the fish in the tank indoors froze into a solid block of ice! We all suffered from exceedingly painful chilblains on fingers and toes.' One school had to spend half of each day in an underground crypt that was damp, draughty, and so dimly lit that the teacher was worried the children would suffer from eye strain. On the days they could not use the crypt they had little choice but to walk the streets; at least it was warmer.[6] Another chilly building was a resort hotel on the north coast of Cornwall which welcomed the arrival of Susan's newly evacuated Hampshire boarding school. The bedrooms may have been better their usual dormitories, but the building was completely unheated. As the winter gales buffeted the coast, the never-ending cold drove the girls to wear their cloaks 'back to front round our waists, with our hands tucked into the hoods', and that was when they were indoors.

Colin in South Norwood found himself in an unusual school building. He had opted not to be evacuated with his school so instead enrolled at Raby Lodge, a private school for boys. Raby Lodge turned out to be an 'eye opener' as it was not quite what he expected. The school was 'a big corrugated shed' in a back garden. The shed consisted of one large room heated by two enormous coke stoves and was run by a formidable elderly lady who kept the boys in line with 'a shout and a scowl which was enough to put fear into the Devil'. Though Colin thought the whole set up 'looked very Dickensian', the school was 'efficient' and the 'pupils got good marks in the examinations'. Colin was happy at Raby Lodge as his teacher was 'a great lady' who, having an understanding of boys, introduced extra-curricular activities such as creating a giant ice slide in the garden during winter to burn off high spirits.

The school that deserved the prize for being the most appropriate war-themed classroom was Taunton School where Tony Harding was a pupil. This school had been joined by two evacuated schools – Eltham College and, in 1940, Kings School from Rochester. It certainly was 'a tight fit' to put three schools into one. Fortunately, Taunton School had a spare building which they converted into three classrooms after they had made room by sawing up the old school aeroplane. The new school building for the evacuees was an aircraft hangar.

I was terrified, no way was I going down there, and much to my father's disgust I screamed and howled the place down.
Julie Gale

Audrey was back in her Sheffield grammar school. This school was next to a large playing field which was now the site of a large battery of anti-aircraft guns, a certain target for the Luftwaffe. A rabbit-warren of underground tunnels, all lined with 'wooden benches running down each side of each corridor', had been dug in the field for the schoolchildren to take shelter in. The warren was not particularly pleasant to sit in, particularly for the pervading smell of wet concrete which never went away, but Audrey found it entertaining to watch the teachers practice the logistics of getting 'several hundred children down there as fast as possible'. Once down in the tunnels all those children were expected to be as quiet as mice, 'but a lot of giggling went on, particularly when the masks were on'. Janet, also in Sheffield and temporarily at nearby Meersbrook Bank School, was not enamoured with the Meersbrook version of air-raid shelters. These were also underground trenches where the children had to 'one by one climb down a small ladder into a dark, damp and spooky tunnel. The only light was little oil lamps and candles and there were spiders and other creepy crawlies'. To Janet, this was a trial in its own right, but what bothered her most was 'the time it took for hundreds of children to climb down the ladder and move along the passage which was only about four feet wide'. This did not instil a great deal of confidence in her when she considered how fast a bomb could drop.

Brian's bomb-damaged West Acton Primary School had a playground shelter which had 'three large compartments and two entrances, the central room had an escape hatch in case each end was blocked with rubble'. At Maurice's school, classes were allocated their individual playground shelter, each one capable of holding 'about forty or so children, plus a couple of teachers'. Young Maurice thought that air-raid shelter training was 'a great adventure', but that soon changed when Bristol became a target area and he had to spend many hours in the school shelters. His school's shelters were built 'with a solid nine inch concrete roof. They measured about forty feet long by twelve feet wide. Inside were several wooden forms for us pupils to sit on and lighting by paraffin hurricane lamps slung from the ceiling, which gave very little light.' Some schools had part-buried shelters like those at Basil's school on Havering Road, Romford. These were 'brick built rectangular surface air-raid shelters with thick concrete roofs . . . they were long narrow subsurface ones with earth piled over the top'. While surface and sub-surface shelters offered some protection for schoolchildren during a raid, Basil 'never really felt safe in them'. A boarding school near Lymington in Hampshire was unfortunate enough to be directly under the bombing flight-path to Southampton. Its sub-surface shelter was partly buried in a wood in the grounds.

Pupil Susan did not like that creepy woodland shelter one bit as it was 'cobwebby, damp and dark, but worse than that was its sinister purpose'. She found that the air-raid drill of 'running through the trees to the strident, insistent sound of the alarm' was in itself a really scary experience; and that was just the practice run.

If a school had underground cellars then these could be used, though it was not always a popular option. Little four-year-old Julie and her parents had a tour of a potential private nursery in Guildford, Surrey. All was going well until the headmistress stopped in her tracks and forthrightly declared, 'And I must tell you Mr and Mrs Cooksey, that we are completely prepared to take shelter in the event of bombing.' This announcement was accompanied by the theatrical gesture of flinging open a large trap door in the floor. The sight of a gaping black hole with stairs falling away into a bottomless dark pit terrified little Julie who promptly 'screamed and howled the place down', much to her parents mortification. Another school that had an air-raid shelter in the cellars was Strand Street School in Grimsby. This school had a rooftop playground from where little schoolboy Tony spent playtimes happily watching exciting scenes such as 'a Spitfire with its cannons flashing, chasing a German aircraft across the rooftops'. As this playground was probably not the safest place to be during an air raid (and perhaps not at any time considering its location), and especially in light of the fact that Grimsby was about to become infamous for being blitzed with booby-trapped butterfly bombs that looked like toys, the school sensibly decided to take refuge in the underground cellars of the building during air raid alerts.

A boys' boarding school in Dulwich was well-equipped for an emergency air-raid situation. The four classroom blocks were 'connected with suitable wires and Morse code buzzers as a means of communication if one or more blocks were damaged'. Being a Boy Scout and a member of the school's Officer Training Corps, schoolboy Alan was one of the boys who manned the signal posts. Fortunately none of the school buildings were bombed, but one stray bomb did land on the 'first slip of the first eleven cricket pitch. This was expertly filled in by the pupils, supervised by the groundsman, making a hump which eventually sank to about level, but for one season slip fielders felt distinctly up in the air'. At the village school on Church Lane, King's Langley, in Hertfordshire, all the pupils crouched beneath their desks when the alert was sounded. The alert – a frantic hammering on the classroom door and shouts of 'Take cover' – were given by spotters. These were senior pupils who took it in turns to stand on watch in the playground, eyes on the roof of the nearby Ovaltine Works from where a flag would be waved to signal incoming enemy aircraft. Pupils at the school, bony knees resting on sheets of brown paper laid beneath their desks for the purpose, bit down onto their coat collars as instructed to prevent tongues being bitten and lungs being blown out if there was an explosion. This at least provided better protection than the suggestions heard in Lincolnshire and Cambridgeshire that children should just hide behind a hedge, or perhaps dress in green school uniform and lie down flat on the grass.[7]

Barbara in North London spent air raids in an underground cloakroom at school. When exams were in progress the pupils had to be as quiet as possible. The coal-hole had been nominated as the exam room which smelt absolutely 'revolting', but school carried on as normal, exams included. Examinations at Basil's Havering Road Infants and Junior School took place in the main hall or the gym despite the air raids, a situation which must have made exams even more unnerving, if that were possible. Risk analysis had been given due wartime consideration: '. . . if a plane was heard coming then they were told to take cover under their desks and additional exam time added'. Considering that examinees might be prone to losing concentration during air raids, 'some allowances were made in marking exam papers'.

Despite the lack of education taking place in school shelters and beneath school desks, at least the schoolchildren had been provided with protection, unlike the unfortunate pupils at twelve-year-old Philip's Chipping Sodbury Grammar School. This school had no air-raid shelter despite being close to the prime target of an aircraft factory which had already suffered fatalities from two heavy raids. The pupils sat in the school corridor during raids, 'backs against the walls and our heads between our knees', a position which might have helped protect them if the windows were blown out but not if the building was blown up. Likewise, Robert, who was now at Gwendraeth Valley Secondary School, South Wales, spent air raids in the school corridor 'for safety's sake', though he had his 'doubts about the wisdom of this, since there were high glass skylights above us'.

There were some schools and pupils who took a defiant, if not blasé, approach to air raids, particularly in the last couple of years of the war when raids were less frequent. For those that had already run the gauntlet of constant alerts, the pattern of raids had become familiar and predictable and therefore alerts were managed differently. The headmaster of St John's School in Caterham Valley, Surrey, placed the importance of uninterrupted education at the fore. He 'did not like the time that the school pupils had to spend in the air-raid shelters when there was a raid in progress', so if there was no aerial activity during an alert he carried on with lessons, using a few older boys like Nigel to 'sit outside and blow whistles when enemy aircraft or gunfire were heard'. Schoolboy Nigel was then accepted at Purley County Grammar School where it was the boys this time that had a devil-may-care approach to air raids. This school had shelters on the edge of the playing field but 'the boys used to bunk out through the emergency exit when the shelter lights failed, and kick a ball about on the field'. The same carefree attitude of air-raid veteran schoolchildren to bombing in 1944 was witnessed by frantic teachers at Terry's school in London who were 'trying to drive reluctant pupils down into the shelters' as there was a V1 in the area. The schoolchildren were caught 'sunbathing on top of the shelters and spotting the buzz-bombs'.

Alan's Dulwich boarding school had 'extensive basements which were reinforced to be used as air-raid shelters if the worst came to the worst' and these were used for the junior pupils. The senior classes, presumably being made of sterner stuff, had to tough it out 'until gunfire was heard'. During one English lesson an enemy fighter plane circled Alan's school, strafing the walls with machine-gun bullets: '"Doggy" Marriot, a former England googly bowler, was taking us for English; he stood at one of the windows shaking his fist and shouting obscenities at the fighter while we lay under our desks laughing – and learning a few new words.' Courage under fire was a quality encouraged in Brian and his fellow pupils in 1944 at St. Clement Dane Grammar School in Hammersmith. Lessons had to continue without interruption right through the many air raids in London. The school kept a spotter on the roof to give the alert if a V1 was heading in their direction, at which point all pupils were to take shelter beneath the limited protection of their desks. Unfortunately there were so many V1 raids, and so much time beneath those desks, that the school was eventually forced to close which was not a bad thing as shortly afterwards 'a flying bomb landed on the sports pavilion, and that was the end of that'.

When the V2 rockets were launched upon Britain there was no warning of their arrival. Basil was now at the Royal Liberty Grammar School, Gidea Park, where education carried on as normal; the school taking its chances along with the rest of southern Britain. On one occasion this school was literally rocked by a nearby V2 explosion during a music lesson in the school hall and 'the school shook and the windows rattled'. The whole class, including Basil, froze: 'For about twenty seconds there was complete silence, nobody said a word or moved. A cold icy feeling passed from my head to my feet. It was the only time I experienced this.' With an air of detachment that could only be acquired from being a Blitz veteran, the music teacher simply paused in his teaching and then 'carried on from where he had stopped'.

When I went to school in the mornings, the first thing we did after the roll was called was to put our arms on our desks and our head on our arms and go to sleep for about thirty minutes or more.

Brian Simpson

The wartime school curriculum focused on the 'three Rs', though the war was brought into the syllabus at all levels just as it was brought into the daily lives of all of Britain's children. In bombed-out Southampton, a town that was suffering from many night-long air raids, the first thing Brian's class did on a morning was to fall sleep. They were allowed a recovery period where they could have a post-air-raid-nap, heads on desks, to enable them to catch up on a missed night's sleep.

Teenage D.J.D. at grammar school in Bromley spent morning assemblies listening to the headmaster 'reading out the names of past pupils who had been killed in action. This was followed later by the names of pupils who had been killed in air raids.' In London, John also had to listen to the all-too-regular announcements on 'who was killed in the previous night's raids', and this was usually followed by penalty time where 'late boys were paraded for their punishment'. While D.J.D. sat in his morning French lesson writing a letter to a French native who replied from the POW camp Stalag XIB in Germany, Jack copied out the daily War Diary from the blackboard and wrote essays on troops in France. War was found in the art room of Chipping Sodbury Grammar School where Philip admired the 'wonderful watercolour paintings of the Blitz' created by a fellow schoolboy who, living in the Cotswolds, 'had a grandstand view' of the Bristol Blitz. The paintings were applauded for their realism. At Newall Infants' School in Otley, West Yorkshire, a visiting policeman instructed the juniors on how to cope with the modern-day danger of bombs and what to do if they found one (the advice being to 'tip-toe away and tell a grown-up'). In Jamie's school in Kent the boys learned traditional wartime family values: 'Teacher had explained that most mothers were frightened and taught her fatherless young war veterans that it was their duty to comfort and support them under bombardment.'

Patriotism was heavily promoted, as was contributing to the war effort. Edward's class in a Whitley Bay infant's school was often taken on a bracing trip to the cliff top to cheer on British submarines. St. John's School in Caterham Valley which Nigel attended, kept 'chickens and rabbits in the school grounds' for the war effort and also spent a lot of time collecting jam jars. At High Street Stoke Newington School, one of Lawrence's teachers kept rabbits for the war effort and this was so strongly encouraged that Lawrence could not help but feel that 'all we ever learned was how to keep rabbits'. Shooting Butts

Boys Boarding School made exemplary use of their extensive seventy-six acres of grounds for the war effort. The school kept 'one sow and twelve piglets, six beehives, numerous rabbits and chickens, one gander and three geese, and a full two acres of land for crops'. Boarder Eric had the choice of joining one of the food ventures for the price of 2/6d, and in addition he could help by 'tree pruning in the forest and potato picking on the farms'. Secondary-school pupils at Devonport High School for Boys in Plymouth were expected to register for war work in the summer holidays, and pupil Desmond's contribution was helping to create allotments for Dig for Victory which 'must have become such a vital part of the war effort that in March 1941 the Luftwaffe dropped a bomb on our allotments!'

Knitting comforts for soldiers and sailors was particularly encouraged, especially if the school had adopted a ship. Joy in Nursling C of E School knitted gloves, scarves and balaclavas for the sailors on board a ship that the school adopted and 'three Naval Officers from this, our adopted ship, came and told us sea stories and thanked us with a gift of a bar of Canadian chocolate!' Another ship, the *Guillemot*, was adopted by Jill's grammar school in Ware and the girls made parcels to send to the ship's crew, though Jill admitted 'we had no idea what to send'. In Betty's grammar school in London the girls were encouraged by their French teacher to knit for the Free French Navy. The girls that took part in this enterprise were easy to spot as their hands were stained blue from the dye in the wool. Betty gallantly persisted at her knitting as she struggled to cast-off her seaman's socks. 'Dad said the sailors would have corns if they were ever finished in time to be worn.' The older girls at Betty's school who knitted pale blue and white woollen sailors' vests, covertly hid messages containing 'their names and addresses in with the finished articles and later received answers'. The same scenario happened in Jill's school where the girls secretly wrote notes to the sailors, slipping them into the parcels, and 'one or two girls received thank you letters . . . but most had no response'; unfortunately their ship sank. In Twickenham, primary school girl Patricia carefully packed the socks and sea-boot socks she had painstakingly knitted from Shetland wool.

She added her special note into her parcel and made a new pen friend: 'I had a letter from a Petty Officer in the Navy. He was mostly stationed in the Far East and we corresponded for quite a while. I never met him.' Boys knitted too. Harding in Taunton knitted 'a balaclava helmet for the Arctic convoys'. Even the infant classes contributed to the war effort. Little William, aged five and too young to handle knitting needles, did his bit by teasing silk cloth at his school in Birkenhead, the fibres being reused for manufacture of parachutes.

The shortages of war had a direct impact on school materials. Paper was in such short supply at Jill's school that 'exercise books and notepads for rough work had to be inspected by a teacher before we were allowed a new one, and every inch of them had to have been used up'. In one school in Scotland the pupils were 'only allowed to fill one page in our drawing books per session and the sums had to be crammed into every inch of the page'. Betty had 'exercise books but had to use the inside covers as paper was in short supply, but shared textbooks, which were very tattered'. Textbooks at John's school were also a rare commodity and those they used were 'very ancient and falling to pieces and totally out of date'. In Evon, Julie enrolled temporarily in the local village school which was so short of paper that the school exercise books were cut in half before being handed out. Margaret had to 'rule lines between lines and write in very small script' that was hard for the teachers to read. Her grammar school exam papers were 'often hand written and duplicated' and often so illegible that the teacher had to copy the questions on the blackboard. The dire shortage of paper and ink was still making an impact on her exams in the days immediately after the war had ended: 'We were given Ordinance Survey maps with no colour! The essence of an OS map is its colour – but obviously Northern Universities Exam Board had a distinct shortage of printing ink.'

The war did provide educational resources and creative inspiration in an unexpected way. Alan made an excellent find on his way to school as he cycled across Wanstead Park one morning: incendiary bomb holes. Armed with a jam jar and a stick he managed to collect some of the phosphorous found in the holes as a present for his teacher:

'. . . this caused little consternation at the time but led to a hurried chemistry lesson on the properties of phosphorous'. Brian's contribution to show-and-tell at school was to bring his exciting find into school. He had live ammunition. It was sensibly confiscated. The woodwork department in Michael's school was certainly not short of raw materials. Their bomb-damaged school proved to be a plentiful source of 'wood from burnt desks and furniture . . . consisting of some good quality hardwood'. The war also provided enthusiasm for those woodwork assignments, such as Frank's project of making his very own Bren gun, of which he was very proud.

> *. . . My worst recollection is that when the lady in charge . . . found it too slow to serve the mashed potatoes with a spoon or scoop, she resorted to dipping her hands into the bowl and slapping a couple of fistfuls onto each plate.*
>
> *Ken Halton*

In Ilkley, North Yorkshire, Ken did not have to return to his billet for lunch anymore as 'a system of communal feeding was to be put into effect' at All Saints School, a service which was to be run by the local branch of the WVS. Ken was not too impressed with the whole school dinner scenario even though he understood that 'the ladies were, of course, working under difficulties and the food was no doubt acceptable under the circumstances'. It was not so much the 'plates and mugs . . . of tinned iron with cutlery of a similar standard' that disillusioned him, but the method of fast-food delivery which entailed one lady serving mashed potato by hand, literally.

Brian was also now having school meals at St. Clement Danes Grammar School in Hammersmith and he found them 'pretty awful', but like Ken he appreciated that 'the kitchen staff worked heroically in poor conditions'. In Sussex, Robert was having his school lunch in Blackburn Hall, a local village hall which had been organized as a venue for lunches 'to help the Londoners' hosts'. Robert's mother was an enthusiastic volunteer who 'threw herself into cooking for eighty or so people each weekday', a task which involved skinning and gutting large numbers of wild rabbits which seemed to be standard fare on the school menu. Barbara often had to eat her pudding of 'prunes and custard, balanced over a sink coated with grey soap suds' in the underground cloakroom during an air raid. The day a doodlebug landed in Stroud Green saw her spending one dinnertime serving rice pudding and jam on tin plates to the homeless who were sat on benches in the playground.

Free milk was available at school and was handed out at break time. The Commons debated in 1943 whether pasteurised milk was the source of TB in London and responsible one year for the 878 cases of chronic diarrhoea in small children. It was suggested that if pasteurised milk was so unhealthy it ought to be sent to Hitler. Instead, it continued to be sent to schools.[8] John liked his 'daily 1/3 pint of full cream milk, sucked through straws (real straw not paper or plastic tubes)' when he was at the village school in Alderbury. In grammar school his free school milk came in 'wide necked, cardboard sealed bottles'. Henri and his friend in East Finchley had the honour of being elected school milk monitors: '. . . this was definitely a license to create noise crashing milk crates both in and out of the classrooms along with distributing and collecting bottles to some thirty-five children'. This responsible position taught Henri such excellent time management that 'with skill the time taken could eat well into the second lesson without encroaching on the bell for the first playtime'.

Not all of those infants drinking their free milk at Henri's primary school could wait until next break to go to the toilet, and the 'phantom tiddlers' resulted in 'numerous steaming smelly pairs of underpants hanging on the big wire fireguard around the large open coal fire warming the classroom in winter!' All across Britain there were many schoolchildren sat in school shelters with their legs crossed, trying to hold on until the end of the air raid rather than face the public humiliation of the dreaded shelter toilet. Maurice's shelter toilet was a typical emergency toilet consisting of a canvas screen that concealed an 'Elsan chemical bucket with no sanitation'. Drinking water was kept right next to the toilet in a 'white, enamel bucket with a lid'. Sound-proofing and ventilation was not available, so everybody knew exactly what someone was doing when enthroned upon the Elsan.

School toilets were not much better. They were always situated outdoors, entailing a walk in the rain or cold of winter. Ann's school had the toilets placed at the far side of the playground, but being girls of a delicate disposition they had the luxury of a 'covered walkway to get to them'. Whitwell House School, which Brian attended when on private evacuation in High Wycombe, would not win any prizes for health and hygiene: 'The toilet was an awful building out in the yard, the smell was so terrible that we boys used to wee in the doorway instead of going right in. We got told off about that.' At John's school the buildings were 'primitive' but it was the toilet which fulfilled the true meaning of the word as 'the urinal area of the "boys" had no roof'. This design did inadvertently provide a popular boys' sport as 'seeing who could p. highest up the wall was a regular contest but I never believed those who said they could go over the top of the wall'. Not surprisingly, this toilet was also placed right across the playground as far away from the main building as possible. In Broad Oak, Robert's school toilet was just as basic. It had no roof and the urinal was a tarred wall. Once again, 'within, at any time of break, could be found two or three naughty urchins competing to see who could pee highest up the wall. Occasionally disaster struck when an angle exceeded the vertical'.

Hygiene was promoted in some schools like Whitehall Place School where Jean was a pupil. The arrival of the weekly mobile Shower Bath in the playground provided a chance to get properly clean, and it was a popular activity 'as it was a way of getting out of lessons'. The Shower Bath arrived by lorry and a 'canvas structure' was put up with 'changing rooms each end, with the shower in the middle section'. A quick way to empty the Shower Bath of lingering children was simply to turn the cold water on as a punishment.

Leading a gang I twice received one stroke of the cane for fighting as compared with three strokes for kissing a girl – a more serious offence.

John Pincham

113

Brian did not confess what his punishment was for piddling in the toilet doorway, but later he briefly attended St Francis School, Horn Lane, in London where 'there was frequent use of the cane which was produced with great relish and a malevolent smile'. The school was not averse to using corporal punishment openly for public humiliation. One boy received a caning on his hands in assembly in front of the whole school: 'Big though he was, he burst into tears and the rest of us were suitably impressed.' Discipline was strict in schools and corporal punishment was considered absolutely necessary, whether it took the form of caning on hands or buttocks or strapping with a split leather strap. Such punishments were logged in the school's Punishment Book. Spanking and slippering with a plimsoll were punishments too minor, and probably too frequent, to log.

At John's primary school 'you were not allowed to speak at all in class except to the teacher and were in trouble if you did'. Catching offenders in maths lessons at his school was aided by placing a girl at the front of the class to call out the names of any talkers. Those who spoke earned a rap across the knuckles with the teacher's pencil. That was quite mild compared to the punishment doled out by the teacher John had when he was aged ten. This class teacher was 'the only man teacher in the school' and was quite handy with the cane. For whispering in a science lesson, John was 'given the cane across the fingers to such a degree that they were blue with bruises and I found it painful to wash my hands for a couple of days after. I got no sympathy from my parents.' Julie's private school in Guildford was particularly harsh when it came to punishment. Hands were beaten with a metal ruler and boys were whipped. One little boy at St Anne's College, London, which had evacuated to Cornwall, had his pockets sewn up after he was found to have concealed marmalade, which he did not like, in them. He was threatened with the punishment of being 'hung from a meat hook in the kitchen' and was often locked up in a dorm during the day.

The headmaster of Britain Street School in Dunstable, an 'energetic man' who was 'known to the boys as Gaffer', was so lightning fast with the cane that he could wallop the hands of eight boys in a record-breaking ten seconds. Bill, whose palms were on the receiving end of the Gaffer's personal record, was rather wishing he had not arrived late to school. At Boultham Junior School in Lincoln, the boys who snuck into the school coal shed one dinner time to play truant were punished for their misdeeds. The headmaster simply locked the door of the dark, rat-infested hole and left them in there for the afternoon. David in Kent was another boy playing truant. As he gaily turned back from the school gates to skip back off home, he was machine-gunned by a low-flying enemy plane, a terrifying shock which saw him fleeing back to the safety of school. Totally traumatized, he confessed the errors of his ways to the Head who decided to forgo punishment as the shaken boy appeared to have finally learnt his lesson. At Barbara's school it was more likely that if a child did not turn up in the morning it meant they might have 'copped it' rather than playing truant. Barbara, living in the thick of London's bombing, was usually found 'tipping more bits of the house in the gutter' from yet another bomb blast.

Girls usually had lighter punishments than boys. While the boys at Britain Street School were being caned at high speed, the girls at this school were punished by being given 'a strict talking to'. Gillian and her friends' punishment for attempting to abscond from their boarding school by riding from Devon to Surrey on captured Dartmoor ponies, was a few days penance on survival rations of bread and water whilst sitting at the babies table. They also had to wear a placard on which was written 'I AM A GOOSE'. Their plight unwittingly elevated them to the status of martyrs in the eyes of the other girls and therefore the punishment was soon abandoned as useless.

In Lightwater School, Surrey, evacuees Terry and his cousin found that the school was 'a modern building and the headmaster had modern ideas', which was quite a change for the London boys who were more used to 'the stick than the carrot' approach to schooling. Here, the Head's philosophy was to reward good work with gold stars, an incentive which saw the two London boys exceed any expectations and become top of the class. This was not common though as it appeared that most headmasters ran their schools using the stick method with no carrot in sight. One such headmaster was at Davies Schoolhouse in Pencader, Carmarthenshire. When the school dentist visited this small Welsh school, one of the big boys was heard screaming in terror. Showing fear in the face of the enemy, or in this case the dentist, was distinctly frowned upon. The Pencader Head, a man who was 'not cursed with the self-doubts of a modern teacher', promptly locked the offending boy in a cupboard under the stairs. This headmaster was a master of ingenuity in psychological deterrents and he gave a modern-day edge to his chastisement of wayward boys: '. . . there was a five hundred pound bomb resting on the carpentry bench to encourage villagers to contribute to some patriotic fund, and this artefact was ideal for his purpose. Offenders would have to lean over this weapon and, thus exposed, receive three strokes of the cane.'

Terry's gold stars were a glimmer of hope that one day there would be a better method of motivation for learning and good behaviour. For many more years corporal punishment would remain an accepted method, and it would be half a century before it was to become completely banned in British education.

Chapter 7

Entertainment

All this!! Our 'never a dull moment' of plane spotting, bomb shrieking, gun blasting, refugee watching, toast making, fire engine and ambulance chasing, as well as troop cheering . . . All this!!

Charles Tyrrell

Role-play copies real life, and so it was the war that was the overriding theme of children's games. In London, Brian, much to his parent's concern, was 'forever constructing buildings with bits of wood and then bombing them to destruction'. His parents were 'dismayed at these warlike tendencies' as their five-year-old 'demolished yet another row of houses'. The games that John and his friends played nearly always involved weapons and fighting, and Donald in Bristol was keen on playing 'dangerous games, simulating war'. The Cowboy and Indian toy figures that Betty and her brother had always played with lay neglected and forgotten. With the new, modern war around them they turned their attention instead to 'violent and aggressive' games with toy German soldiers. Some parents actively encouraged these warlike activities.

Entrepreneurial fathers provided their children with weapons created in the munitions depots of backyard sheds. John was especially pleased when his toolmaker father made him 'a super Tommy gun', and Iain was lucky enough to have an uncle who made a handmade realistic wooden Thompson submachine gun for him. Iain would have been the envy of his friends as he was also provided with a hand-carved 'Short Magazine Lee Enfield rifle *with* bayonet attached'. Nothing though was quite as likely to inspire awe as the real thing. Brian in Southampton had real ammunition at home as his father was in the Home Guard and kept 'a live hand grenade under a bucket in the garden'. Brian was not allowed to play with that so he contented himself with a practice grenade: 'I played with that a lot . . . I even took it to school.' His father, unwilling to fulfil his son's birthday wish for his very own personal grenade, instead gave his twelve-year-old a coveted Commando cosh suitable for close combat. So prized was this possession that Brian still had it sixty years later.

The war brought an unexpected bonanza of new play areas. Michael discovered that 'in Beechen Cliff, off Holloway, one bombed site opened up an entrance into the extensive cave system in the hillside, which we explored with torches and candles'. This made for a novel playground as 'there were caverns and underground waterfalls and some stone-lined tunnels leading to the ancient water supply. Bombs had collapsed some of these.' Bomb sites provided new playgrounds for the intrepid. In Liverpool, one little boy was warned to keep away from these areas: '. . . my mother promised Hell and Damnation if I played in the bombed houses. They had been known to collapse at odd times after a raid, but they were our equivalent of an adventure playground.' Sometimes it was the gruesome that appealed: 'There was a rumour that one of the kids had found a foot shortly after a raid, you never knew your luck.' Another Liverpool boy, Charles, had tremendous fun in the bombed-out buildings of the city: '. . . jumping (without a parachute) from the first floor bedroom windows of bombed houses, or dropping through between the naked floors of the long denuded rooms, sometimes stripping them even barer when more wood was needed to keep our home fire burning.' Richard revelled in the hazards of adventurous play in the 'excellent adventure playgrounds' of London's ruins, oblivious to the what lay beneath his feet: 'It never occurred to us then that people had once lived in what was now a pile of rubble.' Dangerous playgrounds were not just the haunt of boys. Jo, a girl, found Birmingham was one giant playground as she 'rampaged about the city . . . climbing stairs of bombed houses which led nowhere, exploring cellars full of rubble, edging across joists of houses with no floors; all extremely dangerous but exciting'. With their minds occupied with play and having fun, the children on the heath in Dartford probably did not appreciate the irony of playing the 'wall of death' as they raced their bikes around their improvised speedway – the walls of an enormous bomb crater.

> *. . . Nobody I knew had a telephone and I never went in a car until I was eleven (to hospital). This is why films were so popular – seeing such sophisticated items.*
>
> *John Heathcote*

The cinema was tremendously popular, especially the cinema clubs which by 1946 entertained around half a million children. There were, however, major concerns about the detrimental effects of cinema clubs which included inducing mass hysteria, escapism and delinquency. While teachers complained that weekend cinema with its non-educational films completely ruined the discipline instilled in their pupils during the week, MPs debated hard in Parliament to prevent the mental and spiritual decline of the cinema-loving youth.[1] In the meantime, hordes of children jostled and crowded outside cinemas, eager for the highlight of their week – the unrestrained freedom and fun of Saturday-morning cinema shows.

Henri thoroughly enjoyed the whole Saturday morning cinema scene at the Odeon in Hendon. Every weekend without fail he joined his friends in the cinema queue where 'part of the fun would be the rugby style pushing to concertina the queue to squeeze the girls and cause general mayhem'. After paying the sixpence entrance fee the children scrambled for seats until lights out whereupon the 'organ and organist would rise up in front of the screen and we would all sing along to the words on the screen as a bouncing ball was projected over them'. Then the programmes started: '. . . a cartoon, the news, a second feature film, some adverts and then the main feature which invariably was a Western'. It was the Western that the boys liked the most and 'excitement would raise to fever pitch with collective shouting, such as, "Look out Roy [Rogers], he's behind you!"' Several times the cinema manager, 'resplendent in morning tails and white tie', would attempt to regain order by standing on the stage to shout in vain for quiet. In

Wolverhampton, evacuee Derek and his friend also had a ritual of going to the sixpence Saturday morning cinema show. It was always incredibly loud and raucous inside as hundreds of children shrieked and screamed in joyous abandon: '. . . the noise from a cinema full of children was horrendous'. The favourite, a Western series, always ended 'at a cliff hanging moment. You just had to go back next week to see what happened.' In the local flea pits of the Apollo and Adamson cinemas, London boy Charles loved to join the Saturday morning tuppenny rush to see 'The Three Stooges, Will Hay and Moore Marriot, the Marx Brothers and Charlie Chaplin etc., plus umpteen third-rate silent movies all suffering from poor projection and film quality, which made every film appear as if it was continually raining indoors and outdoors'. Lawrence's popular local cinema in Stoke Newington was 'the sort of cinema that when the film show had ended and you were leaving, you had to wade through Monkey Nut shells on your way to the exit'.

When there was an air-raid alert a message was projected across screen to warn cinema goers that a raid was in progress. Patricia never took the slightest bit of notice. Watching the film to the very end had priority and so she would remain firmly seated. Denise was watching *Gone with the Wind* at a cinema in Bath when the film came to a temporary halt to alert the audience to an air raid, allowing time for those who wished to leave. Denise, like Patricia, simply sat tight, determined to watch the rest of the film like many others who were of the same opinion. As there was no way to predict where the bombs would fall, it was probably just as safe inside the cinema as anywhere else unless it took a direct hit.

In the blitzed town of Coventry on a winter's day in 1940, a boy walked with his mother through the devastated town centre and passed a cinema: '. . . one main road had a cinema with the legend "Gone with the Wind" in big bold letters on the front . . . The cinema had gone with the wind, too, only the front was left standing.'

. . . We made collections of shrapnel (from AA guns), bomb splinters, spent MG bullets and burnt out fire bombs, much to the dismay of our mothers.

Frederick Newby

Collecting was a popular childhood occupation, in particular those easily-found souvenirs of war, shrapnel: jagged metal from ack-ack fire, tail fins from incendiary bombs, shell caps, spent bullets, anti-radar Window, an endless list of anything that fell from the sky and could be picked up or dug out of walls, doors or the ground. Children could hardly wait for the morning after an air raid, hot-footing it out of bed to be first on the streets to get the best finds. Jean, with her special collection of twisted metal kept in a large tin, was 'the envy of the street'. Terry's 'prize possession' was a 'solid cone 3.7" in diameter at the base' shell cap, and Basil was on the constant look-out for a real trophy: a brass fuse cap complete with timing markings. These war souvenirs occupied a lot of attention as they were avidly collected, displayed, exchanged and traded. Shrapnel quickly became the main playground currency of 1940s Britain, 'better than money actually'.

Certain pieces were considered to be of particularly high value. Desmond's supreme find was, unfortunately, an unexploded incendiary bomb which 'had made a soft landing in a hedge in Central Park. It was a thick aluminium tube about two inches in diameter and eighteen inches long including four steel tail fins ending in a rounded cap.' He took his souvenir home to inspect and dismantle 'with the devil-may-care courage of boys'. Charles in Liverpool was an enthusiastic collector of his speciality, the incendiary bomb. He was attracted to 'its halo of yellow sulphur, its atrocious smell akin to a stink bomb', and became 'quite unafraid of handling them'. When his father found his secret stash of a live incendiary bomb in the backyard, he got 'a kick up the backside'. Clive acquired his personal incendiary bomb as a present from his father. Sensibly this one had been defused and the appreciative Clive devoted 'some time at the kitchen sink washing silver powder from the inside'. John would have loved to have Clive's incendiary bomb as his ambition was to at least find the tail fin from one. Happily he and his friends discovered their 'Mecca' when they came across a real find: '. . . a lorry load of heavy calibre machine gun bullets dumped in a gravel pit'. Though their liberation of the bullets was thwarted by the timely arrival of a policeman, they did manage to pocket quite a few, but not many which was 'just as well because I recall that there were quite a few duds which had not fired and were still in their cases along with their gunpowder'.

A policeman had to visit several houses in a Leeds suburb to confiscate bullets from schoolchildren who had collected them from a crashed Stirling bomber: 'The school children, alas, reached the wreck before the authorities, and stripped it, particularly of bullets.' David's bother, Jim, spotted 'the local policeman going from house to house that night collecting them – and that when his best friend owned up to having a dozen, he also owned up to hiding them in the fireplace'. His family would no doubt have been alerted to their son's stash of live ammunition when they lit the fire that night. Jim kept tight hold of the flying helmet he 'found' draped over the guns in the rear turret. In London, Brian and his friend Eric acquired some live rounds of ammunition which made for an interesting show-and-tell session in the playground until it was confiscated. The boys 'protested strongly', but were 'reminded us of the dangers of such things'. Later, when Brian went to Worcester College for the Blind in 1946, the dangers of live ammunition were apparent: '. . . there were two boys there who had been blinded and a hand blown off by picking up live hand-grenades'. Nearly 100 child deaths caused by playing with explosives were reported in the newspapers during1942 and 1943.[2]

Crashed aeroplanes were a rich source of souvenirs. Nigel thought he had 'hit the jackpot' when a 'Heinkel 111 disintegrated and crashed on Town End rec.', but he narrowly missed out a find that would have filled his friends with awe. Part of a wingtip had fallen into his garden but by the time he raced home from school it had been confiscated by the RAF. It did not seem at all fair to Nigel considering that his neighbour 'had found the rubber dingy in his garden, which he was allowed to keep'. David in Stockport managed to salvage some mementoes from a German plane that crashed near Torkington. He took home 'some bullets, a cannon shell and a few small pieces of twisted aluminium from the skin of the aircraft'. Typically, curiosity found him performing some DIY experiments with his souvenirs in Dad's garage: 'I put one of the bullets in the vice in the garage and struck the tail with a nail and hammer. Fortunately there was no cartridge attached, only an inert bullet.' A friend of his 'tried this with a live bullet and had to explain to his father why there were holes on the two front doors of the family car, one with torn metal facing inwards and the other with rough edges on the outside'.

The war brought all manner of surprising keepsakes. Charles and his school friends were typical London boys who had the usual collection of shrapnel including 'two-tone blue silk parachute cord from Jerry's airborne landmines', but they came across 'a find which was too good not to be added to our Blitz memorabilia'. Russell Road School boasted an 'elegant gabled façade surmounted with an 18" diameter stone sphere' and, 'following a V1 landing close by, the ball was toppled and buried most of its size in the playground'. The schoolboys managed to free the ball and roll it half a mile down the road to a friend's house where it spent the next decade 'holding down their manhole cover to ensure that a recurring blockage manifested itself by lifting next door's drain cover'. Another major find was delivered from Kent to the home of R.F. His father had procured the souvenir of a 50kg unexploded bomb, defused, which had fallen in the grounds of Hever Castle in Kent. The bomb rode in the back seat of R.F.'s father's car as he made the journey home. On the way, he offered a hitchhiking soldier a lift but the man declined when he saw 'the back seat passenger'. The idea was to turn the bomb into one enormous petrol-lighter and so teenage R.F. began the careful task of dismantling the bomb. The powder from inside the bomb was too good to ignore so was laid in a line up the garden path and lit, producing a satisfying display of flames and smoke. The bomb never did get used as a petrol lighter, but after the war it served as a captivating garden ornament until liberated by a thief. The rag-and-bone man was the prime suspect.

. . . We had already made score marks on its wooden floor by firing homemade bullets the length of the room.
Robert 'Bob' Needham

In public, traditional games were played by children. 'Ducky' Donald and his chums Bongo, Squeezer and Avver, played 'marbles, whips and tops, hoops and sticks, and conkers' and playground favourites 'weak-horse, British bulldog, hide and seek, kick tin and knock-out-Ginger'. Behind the scenes, out of sight from parents, wartime creativity was being added to play. Donald, aged around ten, and his like-minded friends in Bristol who preferred real war-type games, liked to add a little authenticity to their play: 'A favourite was to part fill a lemonade bottle with water, drop a lump of carbide into it and screw the cap down tight. We then lobbed it like a bomb into the hedgerow at Berrow Walk, threw ourselves on the ground like soldiers and waited for the inevitable explosion with showers of broken glass.'

R.J. from Kent was four months older than Donald and those few months gave him an advantage when it came to DIY bomb-making. He and his brothers were budding pyrotechnic specialists who had their own explosives lab, formerly known as Dad's garden shed. Using their ingenuity, they sourced readily available materials for bomb making and fireworks, such as unexploded incendiary bombs which they smuggled into their lab 'where we took off the detonators, tipped out the explosive, and rasped down the magnesium bodies of the bomb canisters'. 'Little John Drums' of potassium permanganate were acquired by convincing the local chemist it was just 'for our mum's hair dye'. Their efforts with copper piping salvaged from bombed buildings and glycerine produced self-igniting bombs which they secretly tested at night by wiring them to the fuse box in the lab and burying them in the garden: 'There was a great c-crump from the bomb exploding underground, followed by lots of earth crashing down on the shed roof and against our high garden fence.' Their escapades would bring all the neighbours out to find out what was going on, but R.J. and his brothers, whistling nonchalantly in feigned innocence, were never suspected. After the all-clear, the boys would surreptitiously sneak back into the garden, hastily fill in the bomb hole and clear away all evidence of their misdemeanours.

As the war progressed, advances in the technology of German ballistic missiles were paralleled in R.J.'s garden laboratory. It was fortunate that the boys' attempts at making rocket fuel were abandoned after a particularly hairy moment: '. . . we gave up when a dangerous experiment with the "horse pistol" that we had made out of copper tubing filled with explosive and lead shot, propelled itself from the school field and onto the roof of the Sullivan's house a few doors up the road from us'. Donald had also progressed. He now experimented with missiles using a jam jar, a candle and 'a 303 round of ammunition nicked by one of our number from the pouch his elder brother, a soldier, had carelessly left lying around the house'. Unfortunately, 'we nearly killed a neighbour, Mrs Porter, as the bullet fired straight through her window into the wall of her room'. Donald, unsurprisingly, got 'well and truly b***ed and grounded'.

At the private school of Trent College, Bob and his friends amused themselves with some serious pyrotechnics by producing rockets made by packing Heinz baked bean tins with cordite sourced from 'piles of aircraft ammunition just lying by the roadside'. This certainly provided some enthusiasm in the school's engineering lab during metalwork sessions as the students rose to the challenge, eagerly soldering fins onto the bean cans. While the cordite produced a satisfying result, it was nothing compared to what was achieved when the cordite propellant was replaced with American grey granules: 'Spontaneous combustion. The rocket exploded with a huge noise. Fortunately we had the sense to take cover at the rear side of the library. The cricket stopped and we spotted white-clad figures starting to run in our direction from Bottom Field, thinking the gas mains had gone up or something. Quick thinking was called for. The rapid response. Excellent military training. We fled right round the college buildings and came uphill panting, behind the last of the cricketers, to see what happened.' As a result of this latest escapade with the DIY super-rocket, the exasperated headmaster 'declared an amnesty if all ammo were deposited in his study while he withdrew to his house, his back turned. So to give him a buzz we left all the ammo on his study carpet in the shape of a huge swastika, shells facing upward at him.'

Chapter 8

War Effort

. . . It was much more interesting going around with a tin hat on . . .

Martin Searle

Fifteen-year-old William was about to have his 'first experience of "power"'. He was on night duty at Thetford Town Hall, tense with anticipation as he waited for the telephone to ring. In front of him was a very important button. When the telephone rang to give news of an incoming air raid, it gave him the authority to press that button which sounded 'a siren which made 8,000 people leap from their beds to seek the various forms of bomb shelter that was available to them'. It was a great feeling. Nine-year-old Ernest was another boy with his eyes glued to a telephone. He sat in his father's ARP office, a brick shelter at the end of his street. For him the thrill was the telephone itself: 'I used to sit in there with him for hours and hours just waiting for the telephone to ring, which was a marvellous thing to me.' Whenever that telephone rang, Ernest would join his father in alerting the neighbourhood to an impending raid. His father would stride importantly down the streets blowing a Scout whistle and escorting people to their shelters. Ernest had the responsibility for carrying the big gas rattle, something he hoped one day to be able to swing around to sound the gas alert. Unfortunately for Ernest, but fortunately for Britain, he never got the chance to use it.

In Acton, Brian enviously watched a group of bloodstained and bandaged teenage boys being helped out of two bomb-blasted houses and loaded onto waiting ambulances. This was an ARP exercise. It all looked like tremendous fun to Brian and his group of young friends:

'. . . how we wished we were big enough to be a "survivor"'. Henry was another boy who cursed his luck at not being a survivor. He took part in a Red Cross exercise as a casualty at Radcliffe Hospital, but after being pronounced dead at the scene he was sent home early. His friend was luckier, '. . . he had a broken arm and he got lunch'. Henry made up for it though; he later joined the Royal Medical Corps as a nursing orderly.

As Henry was an older teenager he was officially old enough to join the ARP, but a little thing like being underage did not thwart keen, patriotic children like schoolboy Martin and his friend who were all too liberal with the truth when asked their age. Their motivation for joining the ARP was that 'it wasn't very pleasant sitting around as a spectator' during the heavy bombing and it was 'much more interesting going around with a tin hat on'; plus, despite their youth, they really did feel that they 'could be of some help'. As bona fide ARP members, the boys assisted in communications and dealt with incendiary bombs. Martin found it to be 'quite an exhilarating experience' and had the satisfaction of feeling 'we were doing something, although it wasn't very much'. For the boys, extinguishing incendiary bombs was something of an adventure even if, on occasion, they 'got the wind up' when one landed too close. As far as Martin was concerned, 'those little things were fine for schoolboys'. However, being in the Civil Defence was potentially full of danger, especially if you lived in bombed-out Birmingham like sixteen-year-old Joyce who was an unofficial member of the ARP. She patrolled the streets of Birmingham with her ARP father and one night, as they were dousing incendiaries, one exploded and her father was seriously injured, losing an eye. Bombs were still falling as the ambulance arrived. Such was the chaos of the Birmingham Blitz that it took three days of searching the hospitals before Joyce's mother found where her husband was.

Teenagers could not join the ARP until they were seventeen, but from the age of fourteen they could volunteer as an ARP messenger. Messengers were recruited in many services because they were needed to provide communication between posts when the telephone lines were down. Fourteen-year-old Jean was an ARP messenger girl in

North London. It was a dangerous job but despite that she cycled through the blacked-out streets every night, an ARP helmet firmly on her head which made her feel 'very important'. Adrian was another fourteen-year-old ARP messenger boy, also in North London. He was issued with 'a tin hat, warrant card and armband' and most importantly, his job was 'to take messages about local bombs and fires to the Fire Station in the Edgware Road at the head of the canal' from the ARP HQ in the crypt of St. Saviours, Warwick Avenue. He cycled as fast as he could through the night, dodging 'bombs, incendiaries and the golden hail of shrapnel that rained down on the streets'. It was a high-risk occupation, right in the thick of air raids with the cacophony of war all around him: '. . . the faint drone of bombers, the thud of explosions and continual anti-aircraft fire and a night sky criss-crossed with searchlight beams – all a tremendous excitement as I pedalled furiously through blacked out streets and sometimes past bombed buildings and fires still burning.'

> *. . . The only weapon we carried was the vicar's World War One 9mm automatic pistol.*
>
> *Frank Colenso*

The Local Defence Volunteers (LDV), later to be called the Home Guard, provided a defensive force of volunteers on the Home Front. The joining age was seventeen and many teenagers volunteered, like Robert in Bath. His duty was to defend the local golf course from German parachutists, patrolling on the back of a motorbike carrying 'a piece of pipe and a bayonet' while the rider was armed with shotgun tied with string slung across his back. The adventure, the responsibility, and the calling to defend your country were a great inspiration for some adventurous younger boys who simply could not wait until they were old enough to do their bit.

Frank was one of a huge crowd at a recreation ground in Falmouth waiting to enlist in the LDV. Even though he was not quite sixteen he was able to join 'a special group' of underage boys who were to become the Cycle Patrol led by the Vicar of Penwerris Parish.

Equipped with armbands and just one vintage pistol between them, the group cycled around the local area at night, keeping their eyes peeled for anything suspicious. Reg in London was fifteen years old but could easily be mistaken for being older as he stood six feet tall, so for him there was 'no problem to become one of the members of the Chelsea platoon of the LDV'. Reg learned valuable skills such as which was 'the most vulnerable parts of a German soldier's body to stick a bayonet', aircraft recognition and map reading, and battle tactics from the Officers who were Great War veterans. His mother, most concerned that her son had placed his life in danger by joining the LDV, wrung her hands anxiously as her son struggled into his 'brand new stiff-as-cardboard army greatcoat', admonishing him to put his scarf on as he set off for a military exercise on Wimbledon Common. Like many volunteers, Reg had a regular full-time job as well as his part-time duties in the Home Guard.

Alan and his friend in Glasgow were even younger than Frank, Reg and Peter. They were only fourteen years old but both were tall for their age and they took full advantage of that. The two boys visited their local Home Guard HQ and 'before we knew what had happened we had both enlisted in the 3rd Battalion Renfrewshire Home Guard under the guidance of the Highlanders'. Alan was not quite sure what his parents would make of his new role in defending the country, suspecting they would be 'rather horrified, but no objections were raised'. Dressed in khaki battledress and armed with American Remington rifles complete with a precious ration of five rounds of .300 ammunition each, the boys were allocated night-time guard duty. This took its toll on the boys as 'having no sleep some nights of course, we went to school and fell sound asleep in our classrooms'. Guarding downed aircraft and digging trenches was very enjoyable and 'we felt we were performing a duty and we enjoyed it – it was all a great excitement to us'. The biggest adventure for Alan happened in May 1941. One night a Messerschmitt 110 flew low, directly over his head, and a figure parachuted out, leaving the plane to crash. Alan rushed home to retrieve his rifle, bayonet and trusty bicycle and pedalled as fast as he could to the site of the wreckage. He found, to his utter astonishment, the German pilot nonchalantly drinking tea in a farmhouse adjacent to the crash site. When army personnel arrived, Alan made himself scarce and the pilot was duly escorted to the tight security of Home Guard HQ, the local Scout hall. A few days later Alan was listening to the BBC News on the wireless when he heard that the German Deputy Führer Rudolf Hess had landed in Scotland: 'I can remember looking at my brother who was also in the Home Guard (he was ten years older than I was) and I distinctly remember my words at the time, "My God, it was him!"' The bike that Alan rode that unforgettable night was his Raleigh Sports bicycle which had been a present for his eleventh birthday. Sixty-four years later Alan was still riding that same bike, every day. His bike achieved celebrity status in the local cycle shops where it became known as the 'Hess Bike'.

> . . . *It was not very pleasant at 3 o'clock in the morning standing on the roof of a seven story mill waiting for bombs to drop.*
>
> *H. Parker*

Ernest crawled on his hands and knees, holding his breath, as he made his way through a smoke-filled tent. This was an essential part of his father's homespun Fire Precautions training programme, a course which involved a tent, a fire, a stirrup pump and small children. Ernest found that 'learning how to put the fire out on us bellies' was 'all fun'. Teams of volunteer fire-watchers were on the alert all over the country, armed with stirrup pumps, shovels and buckets of sand, ready to put out incendiary bomb fires. Their part in Britain's war effort was not only vital to safeguard their homes and neighbourhood, but served to take the burden off the Fire Service which was needed for the major fires which, in war-torn Britain, there were certainly plenty.

Like Ernest, Geoff in Portishead was too young to be on real fire-watching duty but he really liked to put on a tin hat and join the fire-watching team, partly because he felt much safer when he could actually 'see what was happening, and many other people expressed the same opinion'. The other reason was the sheer fun of it as it was 'a joy to be with them and hear what a joke they appeared to make of the whole thing. Anyone would have thought it was the best entertainment possible, instead of a life and death affair.' For Geoff, the positive attitude of the Portishead fire-watchers epitomized the British fighting spirit and confidence in victory. He could not picture fire-watchers in Germany having the same attitude at all: 'I wondered how German fire-watchers passed their time away – not by cracking jokes, I imagine!' In the West Yorkshire town of Bradford, one fifteen-year-old boy did not feel quite so safe when he could see what was happening. He had a bird's-eye view of the city because he had to stand on top of a textile mill, in the dark, during air raids. It was probably not the safest place to be for a young teenager when bombs were dropping, but it was considered a necessary duty, or sacrifice, for employees to protect commercial building against fires started by incendiary bombs. The Bradford teenager undertook his shift armed with his weapons: a stirrup pump, a bucket of water and another of sand. It was not a task he partially enjoyed. After his night shift he was back on the mill floor for work the following morning to do a full day's work.

John was another boy risking his life on the roof of a tall building during air raids. At fourteen years old he was 'issued with the obligatory steel helmet and Fire Guard arm band for the Fire Guards' and trained to extinguish incendiary bombs 'with the piddling jet from a stirrup pump in a bucket of water'. He was quite keen to do his fire-watching duty as it was a welcome break from spending the night sharing a bedroom with his grandmother and her chamber pot. John's task was to patrol the corridors and keep watch on the roof of the six-storey block of flats where he lived. The 'interesting' part was being able to 'watch the searchlights pick out bombers and to see the anti-aircraft shells bursting'. Another fourteen-year-old, William in Ealing, had left school and started his very first job as a Rewind Boy at the Forum Cinema. On the first day he found himself up on the cinema roof during an air raid as his name had been put on the fire-watch roster. William felt happy as not only was he motivated by earning an extra 2/6d pay for this task, but it was 'very exciting . . . watching the searchlight beams dancing around the sky seeking out enemy aircraft and the sight of the exploding shells being sent up into the darkness, and more exciting still was the whistling sound of bits of shrapnel as they plummeted earthwards'. It was a high-risk job, but at the time William was happily oblivious to this until later in life when he would reflect that those on the cinema roof were all 'unaware of how close we'd been to probable death!'

Every teenager was expected do their bit and most, like Dennis in Sheffield, were keen. Dennis had received an official letter stating he had 'to register for civilian service as a part-time messenger in one of the following services: Police – Fire Service – Civil Defence – Home Guard'. He was happy to volunteer because 'being at a very impressionable age of 15½ years, I felt there must be something I could do to help'. Dennis chose the Fire Service because the station, housed in a school, was nearest to home. Dennis's responsibilities were to follow the firefighting appliance (an Austin van towing a trailer pump) and to run messages for the officer in charge. He was issued with a 'full Fire Service Kit, including gas mask and helmet. On the upper part of each sleeve of my tunics was stitched a large white painted letter M. This was to enable the Officer-in-Charge to find me at incidents in the blackout.' When there was a call for motorcycle despatch riders to transfer messages between fire stations, Dennis volunteered as he was very nearly sixteen which was the legal age to ride a motorbike. Very soon he was accepted as a full-time Cadet Fireman Despatch Rider, roaring through the streets of Sheffield on a grey-painted BSA motorbike and 'Riding Shotgun to the red engines'. Dennis felt incredibly proud to serve with the Sheffield National Fire Service, but he did pay a price for his war effort. He later failed an army medical due to 'lung damage caused by smoke inhalation whilst attending fires' which was due to the fact that 'breathing apparatus had not yet been generally introduced into the National Fire Service'.

Once when I called at a house in Capron Road, the woman who answered the door screamed and ran back indoors.

Bill Prentice

General Post Office (GPO) messengers were another group of teenagers doing invaluable war work. At a busy Dover Post Office which was in the line of fire from shells fired across the Channel by German heavy guns, the messengers were regarded as 'a life-line'. Considered to be 'fearless' and 'ruthless', the messengers 'never hesitated taking a telegram whatever conditions were like outside'. The minimum age for GPO messengers was fixed at 14½ years old, but it appeared that some could start working at a relatively young age as part-time messengers or casual workers. Geoff was a 'casual telegram boy from the age of 12' at Portishead Post Office earning '3 pence per mile for all telegrams delivered – riches indeed in those days'.

In Yorkshire, thirteen-year-old Gordon had a part-time after-school job as a GPO telegram boy, riding a 'sit up and beg bicycle'. He wore a 'a small black pillar-box hat with a red trim and a leather belt holding a leather pocket to keep the telegrams safe and to house a pad of reply forms should they be needed', and worked 'every weekday from 5.30pm to 7.30pm, all day Saturday from 9.30am until the last telegraph had been received and delivered, and every other Sunday morning from 10.30am until 12.30pm'. This was in addition to his early-morning paper round and, of course, school. Gordon often had to deliver bad news, usually a telegram, and as a result he often faced 'distraught and heartbroken relatives and soon learned, as well as I could, at the age of thirteen, how to comfort them and what words might be appropriate'. He quickly became proficient 'at making pots of tea for shock' and the situation he found himself in made him 'grow up very quickly'. Gordon's war work had a 'profound and lasting effect' on him which later influenced his decision to become a Methodist Minister.

Fourteen-year-old school leaver Bill had a full-time job as a messenger boy. He was paid a starting rate of 'six shillings and sixpence' for delivering telegrams in Dunstable. He found that delivering red priority stamp telegrams, those that reported of servicemen missing, wounded or killed, an 'unpleasant' part of the job. Frequently, the sight of him on the doorstep, the potential bearer of bad news with a telegram in hand, was a terrible shock. Another fourteen-year-old GPO messenger boy was Bob who worked full-time for St. Nicholas Street Head Post Office in Newcastle. Because Bob was often the bearer of a buff priority War Office envelope containing bad news, when he cycled up a street he attracted a lot of attention: '. . . every eye was boring into me; I was the centre of awesome frightened concern'. Delivering death telegrams placed a heavy burden on his young shoulders and gave him 'a feeling of great sadness', but 'such was the working life of GPO Boy Messengers in World War 2'.

When Bob was sixteen he was old enough to deliver telegrams by motorbike which was 'a great exciting life for any youngster. We were a very rare breed indeed, being one of the very few civilians during the war allowed to ride around on motorcycles.' Despite being 'often hungry, drenched through all day and frozen stiff, bitterly cold in the winter', Bob enjoyed his very important job. The 'daily discipline and work ethic', the camaraderie with the other messengers, and the distinction that being a 'war time Messenger made one a little bit special', gave him a great 'grounding in life'. He summed up the ethos of teenage GPO messengers working on the Home Front: 'We did not attend for work. We attended for duty.' Bob would go on to serve for the Post Office for fifty-six years.

> *I would have given my right arm to fly a Spitfire like some of my brother's friends.*
>
> *John Forbat*

Evacuee John from London sat in 'an old wingless biplane in a farm shed outside Melksham' pretending to be living his dream, which was to be in the RAF. He and his friends would 'climb into the tandem cockpits and waggle the joystick, making engine and machine gun noises until we were hoarse. The nearest I could get to this was in the Air Training Corps which camped us at an RAF station for a fortnight each year.' Many boys aged sixteen to eighteen jumped at the chance to join the new Air Training Corps (ATC) at the beginning of 1941. Younger boys could join if units had space available for junior cadets.

In the new organization's first few months hundreds of thousands of boys raced to become members, eager to be trained as air crew and to get the chance to join those Battle of Britain heroes, the RAF.

The big event for any ATC squadron was the annual camp. Frederick went to the 'Annual Camp at RAF Tranwell (No. 4 Air Gunner School) near Morpeth' where he was shown how to strip and clean Sten guns while waiting for the most exciting part of all, a chance to fly in 'either an Anson or Botha training aircraft'. As part of ATC camp activities, Lawrence got the chance to have a 'thrilling' flight in a De Havilland Dragon airplane, and Tony from 285 Squadron, Purley, had his first flight circling Battersea Power Station in an Airspeed Oxford from Croydon aerodrome. At John's ATC camp he firstly had 'sessions in simulators with real bomb sights, pretending to drop bombs on dimly lit targets, and then finally the real thing: a four-hour operational training flight in a four-engine Stirling bomber'. Dressed in flying suits, the Air Cadets of John's Squadron got a real taste for aerial war in the heavy bomber with 'high altitude bombing on the range and machine gunning at buoys from low altitude over The Wash'. John had the time of his life until 'corkscrew evasive manoeuvres to escape a mock fighter attack half way through this adventure got the better of my stomach and I spent the last two hours retching into the Elsan in the rear'. Afterwards, much to his disappointment, he simply could not face eating his '"flying meal" of two eggs with bacon and sausages' – that coveted rationed egg – which cadets could earn after four hours air time. He might have felt better if he had known that he was not the only cadet to feel a little unwell on an adventurous first flight.

Laurence sat 'strapped in to the mid-upper turret of a real Lancaster complete with guns' and felt very excited. He was a proud cadet of No. 1504 Squadron which camped at RAF Syerston. The heavy bomber that Laurence was flying in had a bomb bay full of 'weeping bombs'. These bombs were considered to be 'too dangerous to transport by land' and the mission was to 'dump them in the sea where they were deemed to be out of harm's way, at least for a while!' Including young teenagers in such missions was perfectly acceptable in wartime Britain, though many years later Laurence would reflect upon the wisdom of this exercise: '. . . the co-pilot reported that at least one of the bombs exploded as it entered the water, a fair measure of the instability of the contents'. Laurence's mother was probably not made aware of this small detail when she 'bravely signed the "blood chit" allowing her plane-mad only child to fly with the RAF'.

It would be at this point that John would sympathise with Laurence who was about to be treated to a display of the aircraft's dexterity, a rite of passage that appeared to be considered good practice. Laurence was oblivious to anything except the controls of the guns in front of him until he suddenly became aware that the ground had disappeared: 'Utter panic – we appeared to be upside down and in imminent danger of ending my life, at which point my breakfast and goodness knows what else became splattered across the guns and turret and I felt impossibly wretched! . . . Eventually a sick-encrusted body was eased out of the disgusting turret and I was laid to rest on the now stable grass where I spent some time panting until I regained some resemblance of normality, and then after some time plodded slowly to the billet to clean myself up. I do not remember what the pilot said but it was not a complementary uttering.'

Laurence's gravity-defying experience was shared by Lancashire boy Maurice who was on his own 'never to be forgotten trip'. He flew in a ten-seater de Havilland Dominie passenger aircraft with other members of his ATC on their way to RAF Halton: 'As the pilot seemed to navigate by following main roads or railway lines, resorting to spiralling down to read the name on the station platform on one occasion, it is perhaps not so surprising that we were sick. Our first task on arrival being to clean up the plane.' Thetford Grammar School's ATC undertook practical flying experience in an aircraft which treated the cadets to high-speed dives. Hanging on tight, Cadet William found he could only support himself with his hands as his feet 'were off the deck and could not be returned until the plane levelled-off'.

Not every parent was happy to see their son join the ATC. Colin's mother's 'face dropped' the first time she saw her fourteen-year-old son in his cadet uniform. One sixteen-year-old, John in Colchester, who wanted to join the RAF had to 'tentatively' ask his father if he could begin by enrolling in the ATC, and Cadet Lawrence felt apprehensive as he prepared for his first flight as 'it was a bit scary because my parents were not keen on me flying'. The high casualty rate among aircrew was well known. At Geoffrey's public school it was 'not uncommon for an old boy to come back dressed in very new Pilot Officer's uniform with his wings and to hear his name read out in chapel only a few weeks later'. The Battle of Britain had shown that air crew had very high casualty rates, but even being an ATC cadet in wartime Britain came with significant risks. Fifty teenage cadets, seven of who were juniors, lost their lives in training accidents from 1942 to 1945. The majority of the fatalities occurred from crashes caused by aircraft malfunctioning or breaking up in the air and collisions with other aircraft. The youngest cadet to lose his life was fourteen-year-old Peter of No. 1180 (Buxton) Squadron who was at ATC camp. He was killed during a training flight in a Lancaster bomber when it crashed; two other cadets, both aged seventeen, also died that day.[1]

> *Once I was 14, a rifle was put into my hands . . .*
> *Geoffrey Patey*

Fourteen-year-old Geoffrey stood smartly to attention in a public school in Northampton, trying to get used to the unaccustomed feel of the rifle in his hands as he listened to 'the time-honoured words of the first lesson in weapon training: "This is the rifle. A soldier's best friend is his rifle."' Geoffrey's lessons included 'drill, weapon training, range firing, battle drills, assault courses and so forth', all necessary preparation for joining the Forces. Joining a military service was the expected, almost unquestioned, direction to take after leaving school: '. . . when we got senior our talk was not of which University we hoped to enter and what we wanted to read, but which Regiment we hoped to join and how to pass Wosby – War Office Selection Board for Commissions.'

Harding's school in Somerset had an Officer Training Corps (OTC), an organization that was soon renamed the Junior Training Corps (JTC), which the boys could join from the age of twelve. Derek, a twelve-year-old at Dulwich College, was the youngest and smallest boy in his school's OTC. The older boys wore current army uniform but, much to his disappointment, Derek had to wear 'the '14 – '18 uniform with puttees'.

The Army Cadet Force was tremendously popular, with 200,000 young boys enrolled by 1942. For those aged fourteen and older, uniform was provided, but not boots. The physical training courses for cadets had to take into account that not every family could afford to buy their sons boots, or have enough clothing coupons to do so, therefore plimsoll-wearing boys were tested separately from booted boys.[2] The Royal Masonic School near Watford had an Army Cadet Corps ('the Third Battalion, the London Rifle Brigade'). Every morning for ten to fifteen minutes the cadets, wearing green forage caps, learned to march fast at 120 paces per minute. They carried rifles 'at the "trail"; we did not "slope arms"'. They used old Lee-Enfield rifles for rifle drill, studied map reading, aircraft recognition, weapon training, and shooting on an outdoor range using .22 bore rifles. On Friday afternoons they had a two- to three-hour training session of defence and invasion manoeuvres which 'usually ended in a glorious mud fight!'

Some schools like City of Bath Boys School offered Air Cadets, Army Cadets and Sea Cadets. Michael, a pupil at Bath, chose the Army Cadets because he was a keen radio enthusiast and the cadets offered him the opportunity to learn 'communications with field radio-telephone sets'. He was also taught 'to drill with and fire the Lee-Enfield .303 rifle' for which he gained marksman status. All of this paved the way to his future service as a Radio Technician in the Royal Signals. For thirteen-year-old Iain, joining the Army Cadets was just the start of what would be a long and fulfilling 36-year career in the army, culminating with service in the Black Watch. Boys could enrol as Sea Cadets from the age of twelve. During the first year of war cadet membership rose from 9,000 to 25,000, and the number doubled again before the end of the war.[3] The President of the Navy Sea Cadets noted that by the time Sea Cadets were aged fifteen they had already had three years of solid training and discipline. Their war efforts at guarding key points, manning signal stations and messenger work were much appreciated.[4] In addition, Sea Cadets were taught semaphore and telegraphy to train as visual signallers and wireless rating. By 1943 this was taught at Portsmouth Harbour aboard the floating HQ of two great vintage ships of the line that had once been part of Nelson's fleet at the Battle of Trafalgar.

> *I felt so smart in my uniform . . .*
> *E. Aynsley*

In Southampton, the adjutant to No. 429 Company Girls Training Corps (GTC), resplendent in a battle blouse and skirt, prepared her cadets for a future career in the services: 'The aim was to make the cadets self-reliant and to be able to cope with many situations and ultimately life in the Services.' She instructed her girls in 'drill with fairly regular Church Parades, Keep Fit and netball and a vast and varied number of visiting speakers covering many subjects including car maintenance, replacing windows, use of stirrup pumps, coping with oil stoves and lamps, and a local doctor who came to deal with health problems'. The adjutant was a firm believer in the observation 'that girls who had been in the GTC were noticeably more fitted to Service life and adapted much more easily'. This was the aim of the new National Association of Training Corps for Girls which offered girls the opportunity to experience pre-military training in a choice of three corps: the GTC, the Girls Nautical Training Corps and the Women's Junior Air Corps.

A teenage girl stood outside the Labour Exchange waiting to sign up for one of the uniformed services. Like all the other girls in her class she chose her local GTC as the Commandant was a teacher at their school. At fourteen years old she felt very proud of being in uniform and she put a lot of effort into learning aircraft recognition, drill, 'how to use a telephone, and do many other things'. She bought her own uniform using her clothing coupons, though if she had been a boy in a service corps she would not have had to. There was a great deal of disappointment that the three girls' corps, initiated by the Government but running under the auspices of a voluntary organization, received no concessions regarding coupons for uniforms. The boys' Air, Sea and Army Cadets were sponsored by Service Departments and therefore received uniforms. Despite many pleas for uniform assistance, the only concession the Girls Corps received from the Government was 30,000 second-hand ATS forage caps.[5]

Elsewhere, girls put their training into practise and this was evident in hospitals around the country. Schoolgirl Jean took exams in 'Home Nursing, Fire Fighting and many others' as a St John Ambulance Brigade cadet in North London. She was also a member of Friern Barnet GTC. Nursing was a popular career choice for girls like Margaret who enrolled in the Cadet Nursing Division of the St John Ambulance in Basingstoke. She spent every Friday evening at Prewett Hospital in 'a specialist unit for badly burned servicemen, mainly sailors and airmen', helping hospital staff by 'cutting up rolls of gauze and folding hundreds of swabs to be used in the operating theatres and wards'. Years later Margaret would train to be a nurse at Westminster Hospital.

In another hospital, this time in London, was fifteen-year-old Denise who had joined her mother's British Red Cross detachment to do some war work in the school holidays. Even though she was a year too young to take her exams to become a full member of the Red Cross, Denise worked as a nurse in Hammersmith Hospital 'as all personnel was severely stretched'. She was 'assigned to quite responsible duties on the surgical side', often resorting 'to surreptitious reference in medical books to ascertain procedures!' Her age and experience were not questioned because of the conditions at the time: 'In emergency situations, no-one questioned one's ability.'

Denise was not the only girl who found she had to assume far more responsibility than she would ordinarily be given if it had not been for the exceptional circumstances of war. Naina took her Red Cross exams aged fifteen: 'My age was never queried but I was told "If you fail on one test or exam in First Aid or nursing, you're out".' On D-Day in

Portsmouth, sixteen-year-old Naina was at Queen Alexander's Hospital nursing 'the first exhaustion cases back from the French beaches' that were arriving by the lorry load. With hundreds of soldiers needing immediate attention, Naina worked non-stop: '. . . stripping dirty clothing from the casualties, taking off old dirty emergency dressings and washing tired faces and bodies. As each one slowly revived, we fed them and administered cold or warm drinks. I don't know how many people we helped but when I had half a minute to stand up straight I looked outside and it was dark.' Naina also nursed the soldiers who were placed in a separate Nissen hut well away from the others. These were German prisoners of war: '. . . about twenty German boys occupied the beds, all about sixteen to eighteen years old. Never in my short life had I seen anything so startling. Painfully thin bodies, long grey hair, sallow skin and eyes popping out of their heads.' Naina was, to the best of her knowledge, 'the youngest nurse in the country to be on official and active duty on D-Day'. Later she would be awarded the Caen Medal for her heroic nursing of injured soldiers.

Girl Guides worked hard for the war effort in many different ways including digging bomb shelters, distributing gas masks, preparing accommodation for evacuees and giving first aid. At the port of Dover, battle-weary troops arriving from the beaches of Dunkirk were helped by a fourteen-year-old Guide who stoked up the pub's boilers and spent three days and nights tirelessly drying their soaked uniforms. In the nearby hospital, Guides from the same troop helped the nurses and wrote letters home for the wounded. Many hospitals were served by Guides: at the Military Base Hospital at Roffey, Sussex, Frank's teenage sister wrote letters for troops who had been wounded after the D-Day landings; in Harrow Hospital Girl Guide June rolled thousands of bandages; and another Guide, Muriel in Chesterfield, industriously provided pillows for hospitals by pulling apart scraps of material to use as stuffing. Other tasks undertaken by Muriel's troop in Chesterfield included collecting 'rose hips to be made into syrup for babies (lots of vitamin C)'. Janet took her 'Guide childcare badge' by helping out in a day nursery, a childcare setting which was 'an innovation' in her area of Sheffield, and she undertook a wide variety of helpful jobs with her troop, from collecting jam jars to potato picking. Being part of a recognized organization also helped girls in many ways. For Jean and her sister it provided a common ground which enabled them to integrate into a different community. Being evacuees, they were experiencing 'a feeling of division' between them, the city girls, and the Surrey country girls, but by joining the local Albury Guides Group the girls found a shared sense of identity and purpose.

A horsebox painted in Guides blue rolled out of blitzed Manchester and headed south. This was a Girl Guide-operated mobile canteen that was travelling around the country from one bombed-out city to another. On its arrival in Chingford, Essex, the ramp was flung down, the stove fired up, and the Guides began serving tea. Their customers were Boy Scouts who were clearing up Chingford's bomb damage after a heavy air raid.[6]

> *So we rode our bikes across Croydon, through the blackout and gunfire regardless if an air raid was on . . .*
>
> *Denis Perry*

The Boy Scouts' motto of 'Be Prepared' was never more apt than when at war. In addition to their many wartime tasks, Scouts volunteered to assist in busy hospital departments; this was probably one of the most emotionally challenging and toughest tasks these young boys had ever faced.

Fourteen-year-old Denis gingerly carried an amputated leg wrapped in a rubber blanket as he headed down the corridor towards the hospital's incinerator. He was at Mayday Hospital, Croydon, where members of the '48th and the 20th Croydon Scout Troops' had volunteered their services. In groups of twelve, the Scouts undertook various duties. Those aged sixteen and over kept a vigil on a 'very high tower as observers overlooking the whole of the hospital's many roofs of the wards'. One of Denis' tasks was to inform relatives if a loved one had been admitted as a serious casualty, and he often had to cycle at full speed through the bomb-blasted, blacked-out streets of Coventry during night raids to deliver these urgent messages. During the heavy raids the ambulances and hospital staff were pushed to their limits and relied upon the Scouts as stretcher-bearers to carry the wounded and dying into the wards. Scouts also helped out on the maternity ward by taking newborn babies in wicker baskets down to the shelters beneath the hospital, while the babies' mothers sheltered beneath their hospital beds.

Other hospitals were also served by Boy Scout troops. East-End teenager Ronald, dressed in a surgical gown, mask and cap, kept his eyes fixed firmly on his wristwatch. He sweated under the strain as accuracy was everything. His role in counting down the seconds for the patient's lumbar puncture was crucial. Ronald was 'Patrol Leader of the 18th Shoreditch (Reginald Bray's Own) Boy Scout Troop' and he was one of a dozen senior Scouts who volunteered for night duty in St. Leonards Hospital in Shoreditch. Even the youngest Scouts had responsible roles. When a bomb hit the council flats and communal air-raid shelter in Nuttall Street opposite the hospital, it was a young Scout who was called upon to administer morphine to those injured in the wreckage. He was the only one small enough to squeeze through a tight gap in the rubble to reach those who were trapped.

Throughout all of his work at the hospital, Ronald found that acting as stretcher-bearer was the hardest task. As the London Blitz continued night after night, Ronald became used to seeing injury and death, all of which was 'far removed from our first aid training' and it certainly made him 'grow up fast', but he never got over the fear that that the next stretcher to come in would be bearing a member of his own family. During one air raid Ronald helped to try and save the life of a baby: 'In the cellar beneath the hospital a doctor treated a baby in arms whose mother had also been injured by flying glass from the blast of a bomb. Handing the baby to me and a pair of tweezers, the doctor instructed me upon how to remove the many pieces of glass embedded in the baby's face and tried to console the mother, who upon being told that her child only had a small chance of survival, pleaded for it to be christened.' With a chaplain present, Boy Scout Ronald became godfather to the baby whose fate would remain forever unknown to him.

Chapter 9

The Bombing of Britain

*Complete blocks of streets just disappeared. One of our school
friends was killed that way and I couldn't even work out where
his street had been, let alone his house.*

Stanley Sloop

War was noise. Living through the London Blitz was to live with a
fear-inducing cacophony of sound: the roar of aeroplanes, the whistle
and crump of bombs, earth-shattering explosions and ear-splitting
blasts, all accompanied by the whoosh and boom of anti-aircraft guns
and the hissing of white-hot shrapnel piercing the air. There was no
getting away from the intensity and sheer volume of it all, and those
who experienced it would never forget it. In Canning Town, Charles
could hear 'the monotonous piston-engine throb of the Heinkels and
Dornier bombers' which he translated as 'Where d'ya want it? Where
d'ya want it?' He found himself 'cowering in terror that was intensified
by the darkness' in his shelter as the war raged above. It was the sounds
of those enemy planes that would forever remain with Frank in
Croydon who would for the rest of his life feel the fear in the pit of
his stomach every single time he heard a bomber in films or on TV.
Tottenhall boy Terry spent night upon night huddled underground,
straining his ears and waiting, like Charles and Frank and thousands
of other children, for the sounds of those German bombers.

The London Blitz started on 7 September 1940 when a force of
nearly 1,000 German aircraft headed across the Channel towards
London. Nine-year-old Colin was in South-East London that day,
visiting his grandparents. Just before teatime he went to the nearby
playing field and was enjoying the spectacle of a barrage balloon being

raised when the bombers reached the city: '. . . high up above a great mass of German bombers and fighters appeared in one long wide column that seemed to go on forever . . . The sky was spotted with black smoke from the anti-aircraft gun fire.' What Colin witnessed was the beginning of a bombing campaign which was to last for fifty-seven consecutive days. The next day, back home in South Norwood, 'a snowstorm' of paper ash fell steadily all day over Colin's garden.

The bombing of London continued night after night. It was raining in Rosemarie's garden, like Colin's, but this time it was not ash but sheets of paper falling from the sky. These were from the nearby Haberdashers School which had been bombed. On Tottenhall Road, Terry watched a river of schoolbooks sail down the road in a tide of water from the firemen's hoses as they battled to save his burning school. In some places the whole landscape changed from the familiar to the unrecognizable and teenage Ronald found 'the sight of heaps of rubble which a short time previously had been a house, factory or school' totally disheartening and 'it was all detrimental to health'. The way an act of destruction could expose the vulnerability of people and their personal lives horrified Jennifer. She was in a taxi on the way to Waterloo Station when she saw that the 'entire end of St. Thomas's Hospital had been blown away'. It was shocking 'to see the beds and bedding hanging from the wreckage'. Rosemarie often passed 'new debris of houses which had been destroyed overnight. On occasion, just the front had been ripped off and it was like looking into an open doll's house with all the rooms in full view.' Joy was rushing home one morning when she saw a 'woman dressed only in satin cami-knickers. I remember distinctly they were edged with the most beautiful coffee-coloured lace. She was covered in soot from head to foot, obviously due to an explosion of some kind . . . she seemed quite unconscious of the fact she wasn't dressed, maybe all her clothes had gone.'

For teenager Joy it was the spectacle of the London Docks burning that created the most vivid images for her. She watched 'one long raid when the sky was completely red, like some unholy cosmic sunset'. The colours of the Blitz also left a strong impression on Barbara whose garden in Crouch End was 'turned orange by the flames. All the autumn flowers were red and orange.' One ten-year-old boy was quite far from the Docks but such was the intensity of the fires that from where he lived the flames 'lit up the sky at night so that it was possible to read a paper just from the glow'. Even from twenty miles away Pamela could 'see the fires and the sky which was the colour of blood . . . we could smell the fires and hear the explosions . . . Whole streets of little houses were wiped out as well as the docks. It was a living nightmare for those brave people.'

Eight-year-old Emily was one of those people. She had recently returned home from evacuation to the London Docklands, just in time for the London Blitz. One night her family headed as usual to their local air-raid shelter where their neighbour would play the piano accordion to help drown out the noise outside. That night the docks went up in flames and the fires spread so wildly that the shelter was soon evacuated, forcing the occupants out into the night to walk through streets lined with burning houses and falling warehouses; and all the time bombs slammed down around. It was bedlam, a 'dreadful time', as an exodus of terrified people fled, all trying to find a place of safety. Evacuated from another shelter once again that same night, Emily was hauled into the back of an ambulance. With men riding on the running boards, the ambulance tore through the streets and at one point was thrown into the air by a bomb blast but landed and raced on, the back doors flying open to reveal a wall of flames behind them. 'The scene was terrifying' and 'all of London seemed to be on fire'. Emily survived that night but she was not totally unscathed; she was left with a life-long fear of fire and enclosed spaces.

Throughout the war, families in London lived with the constant threat of danger. The risk of being bombed-out was high. Teenage Joy and her brother sheltered at home. They were saved by their family's Morrison shelter when their house was demolished by a high explosive bomb. All Joy was aware of was a sound like an 'enormous faucet of water, then total silence and the choking fumes of cordite'. Their father, who had been out watching the raid, had been sucked into the house by the blast and lay in the rubble for two hours with a broken hip and other injuries until an ambulance was available. Joy, her brother and her mother found themselves stood on the street late that night, still in shock, homeless and penniless with only the clothes they stood in and a small brown suitcase of salvaged belongings at their feet. They spent that night sleeping on a stranger's floor. Joy went to work, as usual, the next day. 'Everyone did then you know.'

I remember looking up at the sky from the doorway of our shelter – it was glowing red and I truly believed the fires would spread and swallow us all up.

Donald Williams

To live in Kent during the war was to live on the front line. David lived on the bomber's flight path in Kent. His home was destroyed twice, firstly by a landmine and secondly by lawless people who stripped the ruins of his family's house of all their possessions. David hopelessly dug in the rubble of his home to see what he could salvage but all that remained were a couple of his swimming trophies, bashed and battered, and his Biggles book with a hole blown through it. His mother and little brother were in hospital and so he and his father sought refuge in the Municipal Buildings in Bromley. His father cried in the Rest Centre because 'they only had the nightclothes they wore in the shelter and absolutely nothing else'.

Little Kathleen in Welling, Kent, felt traumatized after one particularly bad night's raid. She climbed out of her shelter to find 'everything flat and burning'. Her home had gone, along with all her beloved pets: her dog, her cat and her goldfish. Her family moved to a new house in Welling but there was no getting away from the war. Shrapnel shot straight through the roof onto her bed, a bomb dropped at the end of the garden and, worst of all, one of her little friends was tragically killed. They had all been leaving for the shelter when the boy slipped his mother's hand to dash back into his house for his comic: '. . . and that was the last I saw of him – just disappeared in an orange flame when the front blew in. To this day I hate the colour orange.' Kathleen was only four years old and the events left her 'a very disturbed and quiet child during this awful time and I had terrible nightmares most every night. I wet myself constantly even at school when I used to mop it up with my beret and can remember just being so unhappy.'

In September 1940 the Southampton Blitz began. One of the worst raids took place in November when the city centre and docks were blasted by hundreds of tons of bombs in a devastating two-night raid. The blaze from the fires could be seen from the coast of France. Ten-year-old Brian was in the city, in the thick of war. He got so used to the bombing that he had developed a routine of not running for the shelter when the siren started; instead he waited for the action to start. One day when he was walking through a Southampton park he came across a surreal scene: the branches of the trees were festooned with clothes. A public shelter by the park had received a direct hit, killing everyone inside. All that was left were their clothes blown into the air. It was impossible to get the bodies out of the collapsed shelter so Brian's father, an air-raid shelter inspector, 'had it filled with lime and concreted over'. Brian walked through the park often and his eyes were always drawn to one item – a coat. 'When the wind blew the sleeve seemed to be waving at you. After a few months it rotted away.'

Crouched behind a wall in Gloucestershire was Philip. The sky overhead was thick with airplanes, an 'awesome' sight of hundreds of enemy planes in V formation heading towards the City of Bristol fifteen miles away. From this distance the bombing sounded like 'one continuous low rumble of thunder that went on for a very long time'. Bristol was repeatedly attacked. Deep in his shelter underground, seven-year-old Donald in Bedminster had his 'eyes tightly closed, hands clenched tight, head hunched down into shoulders and buttocks taut' as a bomb whistled down nearby. 'Oh! What a relief after the explosion when I realized I was still alive!' It was all so frightening to him and 'this was to be repeated hundreds of times over the next couple of years or so. The fear never subsided.' Donald was affected by the obvious anxiety of his parents and neighbours as they lived through the Bristol Blitz; his father was 'worn out' and his mother 'drained'. Just over fifty miles away at a billet in Watchet, panic ensued as the far-off whistling of a bomb was heard. Only one person was indifferent. This was Bristol boy Maurice. He remained as cool as a cucumber and simply wondered 'what all the fuss was about'. One mere distant bomb was nothing compared to what he had experienced. He was a self-proclaimed 'veteran of the Bristol air raids'.

Coventry was destroyed. Barbara played ring-a-ring-a-roses in her garden in London on that moonlit night, a night that would stay in her memory for the sound of the thudding explosions that carried in the air as Coventry was blitzed. Teenage Margaret in Birmingham stood outside her shelter in the bright moonlight, listening to the endless drone of passing bombers heading towards Coventry. Philip was seventy miles away yet he could see the glow in the sky as the city burned. In a West Midlands village five miles from the cathedral city, a thirteen-year-old Coventry schoolboy and his mother watched 'in awe as the sky turned bright red with the glare of all the fires, the flashes of anti-aircraft shells on top of it all'. Fear sat heavily in their stomachs: 'We really never slept that night.' This was the night of 'Moonlight Sonata', 14 November 1940, the Coventry Blitz. Hundreds of German bombers laden with incendiaries, high explosives, oil bombs and landmines, obliterated the city in a ten-hour onslaught.

Coventry had been bombed before this, so many times in fact that 'it all got a bit wearing'. When the Coventry schoolboy was not seeking refuge outside of the city, his nights were usually spent in the shelter with the ground leaping beneath him as the booming of bombs came closer and closer. With the water, gas or electricity frequently cut off, his mother cooked their meals on the open coal fire. He celebrated his thirteenth birthday at home with just a cold sausage sandwich while the bombed-out homeless poured into the Rest Centre at St Margaret's Church Institute where his mother worked. Nothing though could prepare the people of Coventry for the Blitz in November. The devastation to the city was huge: 'Many of the streets were littered with bricks and rubble, burnt and damaged houses everywhere. From the top of Bishop Street I saw that Broadgate was just a heap of smouldering ruins. I later discovered that the cathedral was destroyed. I finally turned into our street, not knowing what I would find. The street was intact, or so it seemed, but every house had holes in the roof caused by flying debris, all windows and many doors had been blown in.'

Brian from London visited Coventry with his mother shortly after the blitz to see his grandparents who were lucky enough to have survived the bombing unscathed. One week later, sitting in their shelter, he could hear Birmingham being bombed. Another boy in Coventry silently sat and watched the light show over Birmingham and could not help but feel 'relieved when it was them and not us'. In Birmingham was Clive. He had spent last week watching the 'orange glow in the sky from the fires' of Coventry being blitzed, and his father had said, 'I'm glad it's not us'. But now it was. Children in different cities, watching each other's homes burn.

More raids. I see dead and injured. After one thirteen-hour raid there is no gas or electricity . . . The centre of Birmingham is a shambles.

Joyce Garvey

Sixteen-year-old Joyce in Birmingham helped a mother give birth by candlelight in a shelter while the bombs pounded down outside. The city had been bombed intermittently since August 1940 but only one week after the Coventry Blitz, Birmingham received its heaviest night of bombing, leaving 20,000 homeless. The children of Birmingham were living in a warzone. Joyce found one Anderson shelter, covered in rubble from a nearby bomb blast, in which five small children were fast asleep – so tired and so used to the raids that they had slept right through the Birmingham Blitz.

Teenage Frederick lived on Birches Green housing estate which was a typical Birmingham battlefield: fires, bombs, explosions, injured neighbours, 'all hell was let loose'. He kept an eye on the moon to gauge the night's raids. A visible moon was a 'Bomber's Moon' which meant that Birmingham 'could be in for a "Big Un" tonight'. He was usually right. Frederick was suffering from the effects of the smoke screen defences which were barrels of burning oil placed on the streets: 'Everyone had sore eyes, coughs; everything in the houses smelled of oil, and the clothes you wore stank for days afterwards. We hated this method of protection, probably because it was self-imposed and caused such distress.' Being close to two main factories, Frederick witnessed many raids that left houses destroyed and people homeless. It was common to see people digging in the rubble and neighbours dead or dying. He helped put out incendiary bomb fires, a highly dangerous task as those incendiaries were armed with explosive charges. He had a narrow escape when one exploded, but his schoolfriend was seriously injured when trying to extinguish one: 'It exploded and blinded him. He was just sixteen.'

The following month was Sheffield's turn. The Sheffield Blitz – Operation Crucible – began on the night of the full moon in December 1940 with two nights of bombing followed by a repeat a couple of nights later which killed several hundred people and left tens of thousands homeless. Dennis' parents had given him his Christmas presents two weeks early because if the heavy bombing continued they might not live to see Christmas Day: '. . . the feeling was so strong that a lot of parents were giving children their Christmas presents early in case the worst happened.' With a heavy heart, Dennis realized that 'most of the city centre . . . was now in ruins and would never be the same again'.

Plymouth was blitzed in 1941. The damage to the city after the attacks was a shock to one fifteen-year-old Plymouth girl. She had a job at Spooners Departmental Store but when she arrived at work she discovered the building had completely disappeared; it had been bombed into oblivion. She wandered around the city feeling 'devastated' as she watched buildings burn. 'The servicemen were in full force, helping the rest of the workers to bring out injured and dead from the smouldering ruin . . . A few of the communal air-raid shelters were sealed (the people inside still sitting upright, killed by air pressure).' Even after the Plymouth Blitz the raids still continued and it was taking its toll on people: '. . . every time the sirens sounded I would begin to shake – most of us had had enough'.

Similar stories were being heard all around the docks and industries of Merseyside which were being repeatedly targeted, as Liverpool boy Charles knew only too well. He spent his nights sheltering with his family, 'huddled into our overcoats in our puny cellar while the might of Hitler's Luftwaffe tried to search us out as a ferret explores the warren for a rabbit'. His vulnerability gave him the overwhelming feeling that the 'bombers were circling above us with our house at the centre of their attention'. He was sheltering in his reinforced cellar listening for that split-second of devastating silence: 'There is a moment of silence between when the whistle stops and the bomb explodes.' Charles had learnt 'to gauge the proximity of the metal ferrets', relying on the sounds he could hear to plot each bomb: '. . . our ears excluded all other noise in the search for the outcome of this bomb's journey. We did not have long to wait as the endless seconds erupted into noise and vibration, as the very earth beneath us shook in protest, and dust cascaded down the walls of the cellar around the perimeter of our steel roof. Mental silence again as we tried to mentally locate where the bomb had come down.' Over the months it all became so routine that Charles became very proficient in auditory bomb-tracking: 'We became somewhat blasé in our reaction to the sound of explosions, blasé, and even expert, in that I suppose we were now able to assess the possible threat of bombs by the sound they made as they tore the air waves to shreds in their descent.'

It was a lot harder for Charles to bomb-track during the May Blitz of 1941 because the noise was overwhelming: 'Imagine yourself sealed into a large metal oil drum which has been surrounded by a posse of deep bass amplifiers so beloved of pop groups today, and each of these amplifiers are pulsating at full volume, and you may get some idea of what life was like in our air-raid shelter during the seven nights of what came to be known as the May Blitz.' The lives of around 370 babies, children and teenagers were known to be lost due to the bombing in the May Blitz, the youngest being a little boy barely a day old.[1] Others would forever remain unidentified or unrecorded.

In 1942 it was the City of Bath's turn. This city was one of the historic towns being attacked in the Baedecker raids. Exeter had just had a two-night raid and Norwich, York and Canterbury were on the list. One thirteen-year-old girl like many others felt 'so frightened and couldn't stop trembling' during the Bath Blitz. Her family sat in peril in their downstairs room where her 'mother, wrapped in a blanket, sat in a chair near the fireplace whilst my brother, wearing greatcoat and tin hat, hunched in the corner'. Michael, aged ten, was also in Bath, at Poets' Corner, and he was absolutely 'terrified'. He and his family hunkered down in their cupboard under the stairs for the night: 'We were two adults and three children in a very small space.' Michael and his family were one of the lucky ones to survive. Hundreds died and many were trapped beneath the ruins of their homes. Identification of casualties was made even more difficult by the effects of a second night of heavy bombing. When St James Church blazed, water from the firemen's hoses flooded the crypt in which had been laid some of those who had died the night before. The water washed the ink from the labels tied to the bodies, and nobody knew who was who or where they had been found.[2]

The morning after the two-night blitz on Bath, teenage Dorothy stepped outside and found a world of destruction and confusion as 'people wandered around in a daze, and one man stumbled by gripping a blanket round his naked body'. Her street was carnage: '. . . the road was alive with snaking pipes as water shot from fractured water mains. Gas pipes, twisted and broken, reared like roaring monsters as gas escaped. The street was flooded and cracked glass had washed into crystal pyramids along the road.' The neighbouring church had 'a mattress pinioned on its steeple . . . It was if a crazed monster had passed by lashing its tail, spraying bricks into large heaps. People buried in the rubble, their arms and legs sticking out, stared like dummies in a clothes shop onto a world of devastation.' The bombing of Bath proved to be traumatic experience for both Dorothy and Michael. Dorothy was left suffering from sleep disturbances and skin rashes, and Michael felt that the blitz was 'a defining moment' where he lost 'the innocence of childhood'.

Tony had his life turned upside down when his town was blitzed and his street was destroyed. In the summer of 1943 the Bomber

County of Lincolnshire experienced its worst raid to date which saw the first mass use of butterfly bombs, 3,000 of which were dropped over Grimsby in 'Devil's Eggs' containers, each bomblet being fitted with a time delay or anti-disturbance fuse. Six-year-old Tony was there that night, staring up at the 'eerie' sight of 'German bombers illuminated by their own flares' as the butterfly bombs were dropped. He would never forget that night because of the 'great devastation in terms of casualties. The slightest movement caused [the butterfly bombs] to explode and clearing them was a veritable nightmare and people were being killed by them until well after the war.' The following month, Grimsby was targeted with high explosives. Tony and his family were squeezed into the cupboard under the stairs when a landmine exploded nearby, destroying dozens of houses including theirs. Tony's last memories of his mother and older sister were of his mother's body protecting him from the collapsing house, and his sister's voice crying out for their mother. 'Both my mother and sister Betty were killed by the explosion. I recall being carried out on a stretcher and looking up thinking how bright the stars appeared.'

My father said, 'That's us gone.' We all nodded.

Brian Simpson

Charles in Canning Town lived in a house that was a sight to see. It was an overcrowded, semi-derelict, bomb-blasted terrace house which was 'frontless with a hastily-rigged tarpaulin covering the bomb damage, whilst the back windows had all been blasted out and covered with heavyweight blackout material battened to the frames'. There was no gas or electricity, just oil lamps for lighting, and for heating a fire was kept burning in the hearth fuelled by wood salvaged from bombed-out buildings. This was by no means unusual. Many children in wartime Britain were living in similar conditions.

Alan's house in Dulwich was in a comparable state of disrepair. The entire roof was covered in tarpaulins to keep out the worst of the weather, and the family slept in the only room still usable – the kitchen. When Alan's mother turned on the oven it was pot luck as to whether they had water or gas coming out of the hob. Brian's family in Southampton kept a tin bath full of water which came in handy as often they had no running water, no electricity and no gas. They had to pull the lino up from the dining room floor to nail onto the windows as there was no glass left in the panes. Barbara's home suffered from bomb blasts too. The 'front windows came into the house, while the back windows went into the garden', and the bare walls, stripped of plaster, were repapered with battlefield maps. Pamela had her house windows broken, then repaired and covered in sticky tape, and then had the lot of them blown out again. Her mother, being practical, merely commented, 'Oh well, I will not have to clean them.'

Ann in Croydon was under strict instructions not to put her hands down the sides of chairs because of the risk of glass splinters. She did not have to worry about her bed though as she did not have a bedroom left to sleep in. All the bedroom ceilings in her house had come down, but the bedrooms were unused anyway as the family slept in the shelter 'so it did not matter'. Ann and her mother were evacuated for their safety, but Ann's father had to remain in Croydon. He lived in the blacked-out kitchen, sleeping fully clothed in a deckchair every night. Frederick's house on the Birches Green Estate had the 'kitchen ceiling down, toilet ceiling down, every window broken, garden fences down'. In addition, everything was covered in thick soot from the chimney. As Frederick surveyed the damage to his home he realized, like Ann, that it really did not matter: 'We were alright, that was the main thing.'

Some children lost their home completely. In London as the Blitz continued, homelessness was on the rise. By the middle of October 1940 there were around a quarter of a million homeless Londoners in desperate circumstances.[3] The Government had chronically over-estimated the number of causalities and underestimated the amount of damage to buildings. Charles in London had more than a houseful after his family took in their 'grandparents, two uncles and the Galvin family, all of whom had been bombed out from further down the road by what was reputed to be the capital's biggest bomb by the size of the crater it made'. Charles, aged around ten, was 'oblivious to their plight' and only when he was older did he realize how difficult it must have been for them. Irene's friend Betty lived next to a railway line and her house had been completely destroyed by a direct hit. Her family had no choice but to 'camp out under the railway arches close to their destroyed home for about two weeks until the local council found them a home'.

Little Terry's house was also hit, but luckily he was at school and his parents were not at home when the bomb hit Highbury Corner Buildings in North London where he lived. The sight of 'broken windows and dirty, dusty bombed buildings' were a common sight in Terry's part of the world, but he still could not believe his eyes when he saw the state of his street: '. . . there were pieces of a trolley bus scattered all over the place, a large pall of dust and debris hung everywhere.' He spent that night with his mother in a school Rest Centre, his mother diligently picking splinters of glass from the bedding she had managed to salvage. Terry's home for the next six weeks was the basement of Multitone Electric of Clerkenwell, the company his parents worked for. Eight-year-old Myfanwy lost her home on a night of the Exeter Blitz in 1942. She lay in the shrubbery with her mother lying on top of her to shield her body, while behind them their house burned to the ground. The following morning they set off walking, still clad in their pyjamas, and eventually found refuge fifteen miles away in Teignmouth where soot from the fires of Exeter blanketed the ground. Thurza in Lewisham no longer had a home. Her house was destroyed just after Christmas 1941. She scavenged with her mother, searching through the debris of their home until they found the remains of their Christmas dinner in the coal cellar: 'The left-over piece of leg of pork was washed under the tap. We blew off the dust from the Christmas cake that Mum had baked and painstakingly iced, then ate them both.' They could not afford to be fussy when all they had left was the clothes they stood up in. Thurza stood forlornly looking up at the only thing remaining of her house which was 'one, lone, narrow column of bricks reaching up bravely into the sky. The wallpaper was still sticking to it and was flapping in the breeze. It was part of the wall that had once been my bedroom. Clinging to it was a small picture of Jesus surrounded by children of various nationalities and colours. It had been above my bed. Written at the top are the words: THE HOPE OF THE WORLD'. Thurza rescued her picture and for the next sixty years, wherever she lived, it remained resolutely above her bed.

In the London docklands, Margaret's family had to move out if they had any chance of surviving. Her grandfather had 'bought a small plot of land in Essex and built what he called a wooden holiday home there – it was not so much a holiday home, more of a two-roomed shed!' This became home for eight of them, with the girls and women sleeping indoors and the men sleeping in tents in the garden. When families like Margaret's evacuated in order to save their lives, their empty family home remained vulnerable – and not just from air raids. Leaving a bomb blasted building unattended, even if it was just a smouldering pile of rubble, was to invite a different type of raider: the chance looter, the career criminal, the desperate and needy, and even children.

Blitz crime was a nation-wide problem. Armed soldiers patrolled Bath after the blitz to stop people plundering the ruins, ARP personnel were on watch in Derby for people 'looking for perks' in derelict houses, and in Soho a gang of young teenagers named The Dead End Kids earned a reputation for pillaging from bombed-out homes.[4] In Kent, David had the ruins of his home 'looted of practically everything. There was no furniture, no pots and pans.' John's house and those of his neighbours in Stuart Road, Wimbledon Park, were severely damaged by bombing in August 1944. John had been sitting on the toilet when he heard the doodlebug's approach and he had bolted to the broom cupboard to shelter with his mother; fortunately both of them survived the explosion. A soldier was posted at the entrance of the Stuart Road to deter looters but John's father and neighbour resolutely camped out in their derelict homes to safeguard their families' belongings. Jill's original family house in Essex was damaged by a landmine blast which had blown off the roof and moved the entire building, but even worse for Jill was not only the fact that a boy was found pilfering the remains of her toy cupboard but her mother let him take what he wanted. Nearly half of the arrests for looting in London during a six-month period of the Blitz were children who succumbed to wartime temptation.[5]

It was not just goods people were after; it could be the house itself. For those who evacuated their property there was a very good chance it would not remain empty for long because it was quite likely to be requisitioned to house a bombed-out family. When Chadwell Heath Local Council issued a request for vacant properties to be handed over for rehousing the unfortunate bombed-out homeless, Jill's family readily agreed and offered their house to let, seeing as they had evacuated to a safer area. There was, however a catch: '. . . it was "for the duration" of the war', so they could not return home after the Blitz. Reclaiming a house, even if the original occupants could prove they wanted to live in it, was problematic if a resident blitz-tenant was not in a position to leave. Frank's family were among many who had little choice but to resort to a court warrant to reclaim their house in Croydon from their tenants at the end of the war. The problem was symptomatic of an underreported chronic housing shortage which resulted in homeless families still living in institutions, Rest Centres, and even air-raid shelters a full year after the war ended.[6]

> *There was no talking, everyone intent on putting one step in front of another. I saw my friend Tom, but we just looked at each other as his family passed by. What could you say?*
>
> *Michael Lee*

While some people chose to evacuate or spend nights in their shelters, there were others who felt their safest option was to take a temporary leave of absence. Vacating a town or city in the evening to spend the night in the neighbouring countryside was an attractive alternative to being blitzed in your sleep or having your home occupied if vacated for a long period. The bonus was that in the morning you could return home (if it was still standing) after a good night's sleep, ready for a day of work, school or shrapnel-collecting. These short-distance semi-evacuees were known as trekkers, and they flooded out of Birmingham, Liverpool, Southampton,

Plymouth, Coventry, Bath – any place that the Luftwaffe was heavily bombing.

Joyce was not happy. It seemed so unfair to her that her 'neighbours started going out of Birmingham at night to escape the raids', leaving their keys with her and asking her to keep an eye on their houses, when she had no choice but to stay. The reason she had to stay was that her family had no transport to enable them to easily leave and return the city. She therefore had to endure the bombing 'night after night and the memories of nights of terror still return'. Another teenage girl watched the trekkers heading out of Plymouth on an evening. She herself was war-weary from the Plymouth Blitz. The trekkers were a 'normal sight' but she found it sad to see these people 'trudging by foot out towards the Moor, with their babies in their prams, and carrying blankets etc. to keep them warm during the long cold nights'.

Charles also watched an exodus of people leaving their dockland homes in Liverpool. These trekkers were certainly a sight to see: 'It began as a trickle along the lengths of Vauxhall, Stanley and Scotland Roads. These trickles converged at Roscommon Street or Prince Edwin Street, and contrary to physics and nature, became a flood flowing uphill; that flood became tidal as it flowed along Netherfield Road South. The tide was humanity. Men, women, children laden with blankets, tents, pots, pans, crockery and food, and an infinite supply of good humour.' Relieved not to be living by the docks like these people, Charles and his mother assisted where they could, giving thirsty trekkers water to drink and offering their doorstep as a temporary pit stop in the weary race to leave Liverpool.

Another household helping trekkers was Joy's family. They lived just four miles outside of the bombed city of Southampton in a village which was a haven for exhausted people seeking shelter. For many months the trekkers walked in their multitudes out of the blitzed city, and Joy's house had an open-door policy: 'Every room in our house had people sleeping. Yes, even in the bathroom.' Even before the Coventry Blitz there were many people trekking out of the war-torn city. One boy was an up-market trekker as his father had been fortunate enough to rent a bedroom in a council house for his wife and son in the village of Fillongley, five miles north of the city. By day they were back home, but in the evenings they bussed to the village for they knew only too well that a night spent in Coventry might well be their last; one family in their street had been killed while sheltering in the basement of a factory on King Richard Street, and the father of one of the boy's schoolfriends was killed when sheltering under a railway bridge. After the first night of the Coventry Blitz, with the roads blocked and the public transport system at a standstill, Coventry's shell-shocked survivors set off on foot for the safety of the countryside. They trekked out of the devastated city in stunned disbelief: 'It seemed as though everyone was walking, in many cases not knowing what they were doing or where they were going.'

Ten-year-old Michael witnessed the procession of trekkers leaving Bath: '. . . a crowd of people walking down Southstoke Road from the top of Entry Hill.' The atmosphere was tangible as these refugees, exiles of bombing, left the city in droves. There was no chatter, no babble amongst the horde which filled the road, just a silent procession of people carrying their luggage and clutching the hands of their children. The trekkers were 'heading slowly and steadily out into the country and away from the nightmare of a city . . . everyone intent on putting one step in front of another'. Michael spotted his friend Tom in the crowd but they did not wave or stop to speak to each other, so dire were the circumstances: '. . . we just looked at each other as his family passed by. What could you say?'

Amongst the Bath Blitz trekkers were Dorothy and her family. They had survived the first night but from the second night they became trekkers; a decision which would save their lives. 'Furniture vans met at the end of the road, and armed with blankets and pillows we clambered aboard and sped out to the hills.' At first this was quite exciting for Dorothy: 'It was like a huge picnic as everyone had brought cocoa and sandwiches, which we ate under the night sky.' Dorothy slept in the luton area of her allotted trekking van, with the adults asleep on the floor. Peering through the curtains at the night sky Dorothy could see 'a world alight with flares, fires and incendiaries'. Bath was under siege and the ground shook, rocking the van as bombs crushed the city. When she returned home to feed her cat and pick up some clean clothes she discovered that all that remained of the house was 'a heap of blackened smouldering timbers'. The distress of living under bombardment, so close to death and destruction, left Dorothy traumatised. She was sent to her aunts to recuperate but being a 'frightened teenager' she could not help 'wetting my bed and my day clothes were often smelly, yet I was never scolded'. Dorothy eventually returned to her original home of London, just in time to 'experience further wartime terrors' as she was about to come face to face with Hitler's latest weapons of destruction: flying bombs and long-range ballistic missiles.

Chapter 10

The End

Mother had a codicil to the usual rules: '. . . and if you hear a V-bomb coming, Jamie, you know you can leave the table without permission.'

Edward 'Jamie' James

One night in June 1944, Barbara watched what looked like a tiny plane flying in a straight line across the sky, followed by several others. As if in warning, 'the picture of The Madonna and Child by Raphael, which hung between our beds, slid quietly off the wall – not a good sign'. It was indeed a fitting portent as London was being attacked by a long-range weapon with a silhouette shaped like a flying crucifix, a weapon with a sound that became known as the Devil's Organ Pipe. These pilotless planes were the latest in German technology and became known by different names: the flying bomb, buzz bomb, diver, the V1 for vengeance weapon, or simply the doodlebug. Three and a half weeks after the first doodlebug landed, nearly 3,000 civilians lay dead, 8,000 were hospitalized and many more untold thousands needed treatment for minor injuries. Before the war ended, the fatalities would double.[1]

Doodlebugs were launched from France and Holland with one directive: to break Britain. They were produced in underground factories using slave labour, and not just one or two but hundreds of these bombs could be launched in just one night. These bombs were not designed to hit specific targets; 'the general direction of London was good enough.' London, Bristol and the South Coast were the targets of these bombs, but anyone living in the Doodlebug Triangle of Dover, London and Southampton was at high risk. The first flying bomb attacks were not a complete surprise to the Government, but they were to the general public. People speculated wildly as to what these new things were and 'rumours spread of all kinds of bizarre things until we were told the truth'. Alan heard that they might even be 'suicide bombers'.

Pamela in Kent lived in 'Flying Bomb Alley', the bomb highway over which the doodlebugs passed. She was, however, in London's Hyde Park when she saw her first doodlebug. It had a distinctive sound. Colin thought they sounded strange, 'as if it was only firing on a few cylinders and all the bearings had worn out'. Six-year-old John in North London heard it as the 'hideous hum of this aeroplane-with-a-difference', and Jill thought it sounded like a 'rather rough old lorry struggling up a hill'. Other children likened the sound to that of a motorbike. While a doodlebug was noisily motoring its way overhead there was no danger yet; it was when the engine cut out at a predetermined point that it became lethal as at that moment it would point to earth and drop like a stone – a stone with an explosive warhead. It was therefore not the noise of the Devil's Organ Pipe that struck terror into the pit of your stomach, but the sudden heart-stopping silence.

Children listened to the doodlebugs chugging overhead, waiting for that sudden silence, knowing at that point they had barely eleven seconds to run and hide. It was those seconds of silence, that final warning, that was the reason June in Middlesex hated catching the bus to school as she could not hear the doodlebugs' flight over the noise of the bus engine. She preferred to go by bicycle, ears ever on the alert, because at least then she could hear the doodlebug's engine cutting out and dive for cover: 'On a cycle I knew where all the ditches were.' In Kensington the unmistakable sound of a doodlebug was getting closer, and then the noise stopped. The queue waiting for the No. 49 bus outside Gloucester Road Underground Station stood frozen to the spot: 'In a typically British way, no-one wanted to be the first to run.' Reaching crisis point, the queue suddenly broke and ran as one to the Tube entrance just before the inevitable explosion. As soon as it was over everyone brushed themselves down and filed out to re-form their queue again as if nothing out of the ordinary had happened. Londoners were, by now, veterans of war.

Another London bus was picking up passengers by St James Park. Eleven-year-old Betty and her mother were aboard, both keen to get home after a hair-raising trip to the theatre where the theatre shook from a doodlebug explosion. It was December and a bitter wind howled through the bus windows which had no glass as it had all been blown out by the blast. The bus driver had stopped briefly to sweep away the glass before continuing stoically on his way to pick up his passengers: 'This was the way people continued to live their daily lives, which was to carry on as usual.' Terry could confirm this determined British attitude. He was on another London bus. This one had windows fortified with 'green gauze intended to protect against flying glass, and in each panel was just one section six inches long and three inches deep for passengers to peer through to see where they were'. Riding these buses with the world blinkered from sight was probably not a bad idea, for when Terry peeped through the gap in the window he had a shock: 'To my amazement there was the dark shape of a flying bomb about half a mile away, running parallel with the bus but much faster.' Those London buses running without fail through missile-city epitomized the spirit of wartime Britain.

In Acton, London, ten-year-old Brian lay face down in the gutter of Saxon Road. He was obediently following the explicit instruction he had been given on what to do if you heard a doodlebug nearby: '. . . you had to lie down in the road'. The menace was so frequent, day and night, that he was beginning to find that it was all 'very hard on the nerves', not to mention his clothes. Londoner Alan, aged eleven, had quickly developed doodlebug survival instincts: 'One almost subconsciously while walking along the street kept an eye open for substantial brick walls or entries between buildings to lie down against or in, at a second's notice.' In Surrey, Joan was amazed at the sheer amount of these doodlebugs flying overhead and one day she counted '120 of them flying over in one hour'. Teenage Patricia in Twickenham was more disturbed by these new bombs than she had been by the high explosive bombs of the Blitz. The sheer destruction caused by this new weapon was 'the true face of war as we had never seen it'. Every building seemed to be windowless and the streets were covered in rubble. As the doodlebugs growled overhead, she lay in bed clinging to her mother, 'convinced I was going to die'. Another London teenager, Muriel, felt differently. She had a fatalistic attitude to the danger of doodlebugs: '. . . we did not worry unduly about these bombs. It was, I suppose, like the Blitz, if you "copped one" that was it.' One doodlebug passed nearby while she was sitting her geography exam. She simply kept on writing.

The doodlebug warning siren in Frank's city of Eastbourne was called the Cuckoo as it warbled 'with cut outs every couple of seconds'. It was not very reliable as when at school Frank seemed to be either running with his class towards the shelters with a doodlebug flying overhead or crouched under a desk at the teacher's command of 'Down!'. Even those who could not hear a doodlebug could feel it, and this was confirmed by Frank's deaf mother who could 'feel the engines by the vibrations of the house as they flew over'. There were so many doodlebugs triggering so many air-raid warnings that people in London often got confused as to the state of play and therefore they began to ignore the alerts, relying instead on what they could hear and see in the sky. In Basil's street in Romford it was not the sirens that gave the doodlebug alerts, it was the children. Perched on the doorstep of his Anderson shelter during yet another lengthy air raid, Basil had a home-made bamboo-and-pea whistle at the ready. He scanned the sky, hoping to be the first to spot a doodlebug so he could blow his whistle to alert the mothers who were indoors doing their household chores. He was in hot competition with other children further up the road. They were his doodlebug-spotting rivals as every one of them wanted the kudos of being the first to blow their whistle. In the town of Strood, Kent, four-year-old Roger's air-raid alert station was his garden gate where he would sit on his little red tricycle, listening for the sound of approaching doodlebugs. Should he hear one he would frantically pedal back down the garden path to warn Mother.

Teenage Jeff was a trained industrial spotter at Bugsbys Reach, Greenwich, in 1944. The Alarm within the Alert was an air-raid warning system to alert factories when incoming enemy were within a fifteen-mile radius and heading their way. This lessened the indeterminable amount of time factory workers had to spend in shelters during air raids when the action might be elsewhere. As a spotter, Jeff certainly witnessed some erratic doodlebugs, including ones which glided in low, others that suddenly banked sideways, and one which suddenly climbed vertically then looped back down before hitting the ground. One of Jeff's ATC friends was killed when a doodlebug hit his home on Fursfield Road. During the funeral procession a doodlebug landed half a mile away with a deafening, ground-shaking detonation, destroying Charlton Railway Station and surrounding shops. The cortege had barely made it to the graveside before another doodlebug appeared. This one headed straight towards them but suddenly curved away, hitting Shooters Hill in full view of the mourners who 'silently watched in horror as many houses were reduced to rubble by the explosion'. For Jeff, experienced as he was in spotting, it was a day 'hard to forget'.

Some children could not help but feel in awe of this new flying bomb technology. Teenage Irene appreciated that these doodlebugs were 'amazing things to watch in daylight as they hurtled across the skyline, flames pouring from the back of them'.[2] In Kent, pyrotechnic expert and rocket entrepreneur R.J., aged ten, was in his element. To him, the flying bombs were 'beautiful inventions and were the pinnacle of excitement to observe with the deep-throated throbbing sound of their liquid oxygen [sic] engine; the suspense of waiting for the motor to cut out; and the uncertainty of how and where they would glide before hitting the ground.' He could not believe his luck when a faulty doodlebug was found 'sticking out of the roof of No. 236 Northumberland Avenue'. He 'desperately wanted to get a closer look and hopefully some sample bits', but was thwarted by the authorities who sensibly evacuated the area. The technology may have been novel, but after five years of war the devastation wrecked by these vengeance weapons was nothing new in a childhood in which war was normal.

Allied aircraft were successfully bombing the doodlebug launch sites and railway links, and unbeknown to little Barbara and her sister, Margaret, in Wales, their brother was one of many heading towards those sites in a Stirling bomber helping to save Britain.[3] It was not to end yet. Just over 6,000 people in Britain would be killed by doodlebugs from June 1944 to March 1945, but more were about to face Germany's newer, better, faster vengeance weapon. This was the V2.

Fourteen-year-old Ron and his friends who had been playing football on the sports ground by Barnes Bridge were heading home for tea early one September evening in 1944. None of them were expecting what happened next: '. . . there was the most astounding noise that I can only describe as a thunderous whiplash type of crack that filled our heads with a painful crescendo of sound. To this day I can still recall that noise . . . jarring our teeth with an almost unbearable sound that scrambled our eardrums and stopped all our comprehension.' This was totally unlike anything they had experienced in the Blitz as there was 'no blast wind and there had certainly been no air-raid sirens' and the noise, unlike a normal explosion, did 'not seem "warlike"'. Returning home, the streets were full of Service vehicles heading for the Chiswick area. Rumour had it that a gas main had blown. What Ron had witnessed was in fact Britain's first V2 attack, a ballistic missile travelling at supersonic speed from the stratosphere which plunged to earth, hitting Staveley Road in Chiswick. Launched from Holland, the 760kg of Amatol high explosive in the warhead had blown a crater 35ft wide, demolishing nearly a dozen houses and blast-damaging over 500 others.

Unlike the doodlebugs, there was no warning of the V2's arrival, no time to run for cover. They could not be stopped by guns, aeroplanes or barrage balloons, and the only defence was to destroy or capture them at the launching sites. These weapons were not given a nickname; they were far too serious for that. When a V2 arrived the first sound to be heard was the explosion immediately followed by a sonic boom as the missile broke the sound barrier. If you could hear a V2, then it had missed you. Over a period of six months around 1,000 of these super rockets landed in Britain, killing nearly 3,000 people.[4]

V2s frightened Pamela and Irene far more than doodlebugs, and Jill was 'more unsettled by the thought of being blown up by a V2 than anything else in the war'. Muriel thought they were 'something else again' but accepted that 'it was a case of if you were unlucky that was it'. Not everyone was as stoic. Dorothy was 'terrified' but as she was about to start her new job she felt she must put on a brave face like everyone else and 'appear grown-up and not worried'. Some people like Alan found the doodlebugs more terrifying than the V2, preferring not to have that dreadful knowledge that a bomb was descending: '. . . the V1s were worse, because of the extreme mental pressure when one heard one approaching, which just worsened when the engine cut. Then, if it was really close, one could actually hear a swishing as it glided to its final impact.' With the V2, you could not even run for shelter.

Schoolboy Peter's first experience of a near miss from a V2 was a 'sudden total blackness pierced by a bright red flash'. The bomb had landed very close to Tottenham Grammar School and a black cloud of smoke billowed over the school buildings. 'In the event, two boys lost their lives as a result of injuries received and a third boy lost an arm', but had the V2 'fallen fifty yards to the south it would have destroyed the school and most of the pupils'. The school children behaved with such calmness during the calamity, showing 'no panic and this is confirmed by contemporary newspaper reports'. However, the danger to children lay not only in the physical threat of bombing during this final year of war, but the chaotic state of affairs it engendered. This was never more apparent than the case of one little boy who was handed in to a police station in the East End of London in March 1945. According to a member of the public, the child had been abandoned by a local family. Subsequently the police closed the case and the little boy was placed for adoption, overlooking the fact that he had been reported missing by his distressed parents in Plymouth. In 1948, when the boy was finally identified and reunited with his parents, an enquiry was held as to the failure of the system. The blame was laid on the conditions caused by rockets and missile attacks which made police inquiries difficult during this period.[5]

THE END

At the end of March 1945 the very last V2 weapons were fired on Britain. One in particular left many dead. The evening before, teenage Stanley had been to the Brady Boys Club in London's East End and had escorted a girl back to her home in the tenement blocks of Hughes Mansions, Stepney, where many families lived. The next morning Stanley's mother 'heard an explosion followed by a dark cloud which drifted in her direction'. This was not a cloud of smoke or dust, it was millions upon millions of feathers – 'feathers from the mattresses of those who had lived, and died, in Hughes Mansions'. The rocket had landed directly in the middle block of the tenements, killing 134 people. That same afternoon another one landed in Orpington, flattening fifteen houses and killing an elderly lady. The next morning a few doodlebugs were belatedly fired at Britain just before the last rocket and flying-bomb launch sites were overrun by the advancing Allied armies. By lunchtime there was a strange silence. No throb of German planes, no whistling of bombs, no chugging doodlebugs and no sonic booms. After six years of war, the bombing of Britain was over.

> *I remember asking my mother, 'Whatever will the news on the wireless be about when there isn't a war?' 'Oh, about the doings of the Royal Family and things like that, I expect,' she said.*
>
> *M. Green*

At an infant school in Buckingham, the teachers prepared a surprise for their pupils. Tables were covered with newspaper and laid with sugar-paper and brand-new paints that had been magically produced from the stock cupboard for this special occasion. It was 8 May 1945, Victory in Europe (VE) Day. The children spent the afternoon painting multiple Union Jacks. At her school in Yorkshire, Julia put the finishing touches to her VE Day booklet with a 'picture on every page and ending with "God save the King and Queen"'. As she walked home from school that afternoon she saw the forested hill of Otley Chevin being decorated with a 'giant V shape made with torches'.

169

Clutched in her hand was a special thank-you letter from King George which had been sent to every schoolchild in the country. Ten miles away, Ernest walked home from his school in Leeds with a big ball of chalk in his hand. He wrote the letters VE from one side of the road to the other, all the way up Belle Isle Road, dodging the trams as he chalked over the tram lines. He was looking forward to the big street party that was going to be held in his cul-de-sac later.

Also in Leeds were Mavis and her siblings. They were not looking forward to their street party as they could not attend; they could not afford the entrance fee of sixpence per person. They had been living in abject poverty after their father died in 1940 on board the troopship *Lancastria*. Mavis's mother and her four sisters 'never had any money to be properly fed, never mind parties'. Fortunately their plight did not go unnoticed by a kind benefactor who 'sent five separate envelopes with the sixpences in for us'. Things were rather different at Irene's street party in London. Rather than charging a fee to attend it was decided that money should be freely given to every child who lived in the road. The local taxi driver sat at a table and handed out a sixpence to every child in the street.

Residents all across Britain organized victory street parties. Bunting and flags were hung from house to house, hoarded rations were prepared into feasts, and tables and chairs were dragged out into roads. Terry had a big Union Jack flag complete with tassels which he had used at Scout parades, and he proudly hung it up for display; 'it made a brave sight'. John also appreciated all the flags hung from all the upstairs windows in his street in South Wimbledon, and especially the rows of coloured light bulbs that someone had covertly plugged into a street lamp. In Kipling Avenue in Bath, a man quietly wired his film projector to a convenient street lamp so he could project cartoons of Mickey Mouse and Felix the Cat onto a house wall for the local children. In Irene's street in Mitcham, organization of the street party was planned to perfection by a committee formed by the women of the street. Trestle tables and chairs were placed in the middle of the road, spread with table cloths and decorated with hand-picked flowers. Finally, platters laden with food were miraculously produced from busy kitchens as mothers conjured up a banquet from their rations. While Terry's mother served cakes and jelly in Tottenhall, a pub in Sunbury-on-Thames offered its customers free swan sandwiches. An eight-year-old boy who lived near the pub was suspicious because the resident aggressive swan, which 'had for some time terrorised people by hiding near a bakery then attacking passing shoppers and snatching food from baskets', had curiously disappeared.

As children everywhere were scrubbed clean and dressed in their best clothes, Shirley's mother put the finishing touches to her daughter's Victory dress which she had 'made out of red parachute silk trimmed with blue and white braid around the bottom, sleeves and collar'. Five-year-old Madeleine in Walton-on-Thames dressed in her 'best blue silk dress and silver cross and chain', while Irene proudly wore not only her very best dress but her brand new 'wooden soled sandals I was so proud of'. To Irene's astonishment, one of the elderly church ladies 'of staid and sober habits' turned up resplendent in an eye-catching red dress and was later seen leading the conga up the street.[6]

Victory bonfires blazed all over Britain, so much so that the Fire Service was kept busy. A fire engine stood on standby in Jill's street because the bonfire next to the pub had begun to get out of control and the 'paintwork on the pub started to blister'. Twelve-year-old Brian proudly rang the gas bell in his street in Acton before he headed up to the massive bonfire that blazed away by the Cox & Danks. Anything that could be burnt was contributed, and this included 'two pianos [and] a hundred yards of fencing belonging to a factory'. Another bonfire, this time in his street, was lit and was so fierce it 'burned all the tarmac down to the concrete base, this bare patch remained for ages afterwards'. In Canning Town, Charles's street bonfire would be one to remember. His street had not organized a party as there were 'just thirteen bomb blasted houses left standing out of an original 200-odd so that a party in South Molton Road was out of the question'. This did not deter Charles and his teenage friends who, 'having graduated in inventiveness through our Blitz-education', decided to create the '"mother and father" of all street bonfires'. The vast amount of wood available from bombed out houses, combined with a few old horse carts from the bombed-out remains of Fox's hauliers yard, made for a monster fire. It burned 'for about three days and threatened to cause as much damage to the street as had the Germans'.

In Liverpool, one young boy was a bit confused as to what was going on as he had thought a bonfire was actually 'bomb-fire', an easy mistake to make when bomb-fires were what he had grown up with. If he had visited some of the party bonfires like Charles' that night, he would very likely remain convinced that they were indeed bomb-fires. It was at Charles' bonfire-to-beat-all-bonfires that a new source of pyrotechnics was discovered by the adventurous boys. The 'large sheets of asbestos which the War Damage Repair building teams had used after the 40/43 Blitz', were thrown on top of their inferno and proved to 'explode with a large bang; the inherent danger of this was completely lost on us carefree lads'. The roads of Acton and Canning Town were not the only ones scarred by bonfires that night. In Lambeth, the council was left reeling when faced with an astronomical repair bill of £2,750 to repair the roads damaged by their borough's victory infernos.[7]

Many victory bonfires were accompanied by firework displays. At David's bonfire in Stockport someone produced 'rockets and twopenny bangers . . . set off under dustbin lids for added effect'. The bonfires that Frank attended were crowd-gatherers due to the use of 'many illicit flares and thunder flashes which no longer had military applications'. In Luton, a town that 'went mad' celebrating, a schoolboy spotted that Currys had fireworks for sale, but the shop was in chaos: '. . . the police lost control of the crowd and people were filing through the shop, many not paying. What days.' A few miles away, the explosives (which 'were lightly called fireworks') at the Dunstable celebrations attracted a lot of attention: '. . . one of them blew a hole in the pavement outside Gibbards the chandlers on the High Street', not that such a thing fazed messenger boy Bill who was having a whale of a time. He caroused 'arm in arm, six abreast, down Luton Road' until the early hours of the morning.

VE Day in St Albans was a riot, literally. Sixteen-year-old Robin was one face in a huge crowd that gathered in the market place, 'all waiting for something to happen'. Sadly, the Town Council had not organized anything, an oversight which did not go down too well with the locals. The boisterous crowd provided their own entertainment by linking arms and singing, pianos were put out on the streets, and the pubs threw open their doors to supply food and drink. It did not go unnoticed that there appeared to be an exclusive private party at the Town Hall and this tipped the balance, causing stirrings of unrest amongst the crowd. The riot started with a bystander leaping on top of the car park attendant's hut shouting, 'Get the Town Hall', which prompted a surge towards the building. A few intrepid sailors started to scale the front of the Town Hall and a 'young hot-head' on a motorbike attempted to pull down the big door with a length of rope tied to his motorbike. After some car rocking and booing, an impromptu bonfire was started in the middle of the street with the car park attendant's hut thrown on top as a sacrificial Council Guy. This was brought to the attention of the Fire Service who dutifully arrived to put out the fire. Their presence was not appreciated and the locals gave vent to their feelings by retaliating with lumps of earth from the flower displays. Once the Fire Brigade had retreated, the bonfire party continued and revellers celebrated uninterrupted throughout the night. When dawn broke, the locals of St Albans returned to their homes, 'exhausted and happy'.

In contrast to events in St Albans, the Mayor of Guildford made sure he kept his town happy as he had organized a town party. Having finished his speech from the balcony of the town hall, he 'pointed with a flourish to the hill called the Hoggs Back which overlooks Guildford and cried, "There will be a bonfire on the hill tonight, bring everything we can burn."' Julie was amongst the appreciative Guildford crowd that 'cheered and cheered'. That night, hundreds of Guildford residents threw their blackout blinds on the Hoggs Back bonfire and danced the conga by firelight.

The City of London hosted a magnificent public celebration. Frank got up early to catch the 6.20am train to London where the crowds were already huge. Little Madeleine, in her blue silk dress, sat on someone's shoulders by the George pub and saw before her a 'sea of heads . . . and what seemed like hundreds of people waving flags, singing, dancing, hugging and some even crying'. Brightly-coloured flags, patriotic bunting and streamers gaily adorned the buildings as bands played the National Anthem to announce the arrival of the Royal Family: 'We couldn't believe our eyes, but there waving and smiling were King George VI, Queen Elizabeth and the Princesses Elizabeth and Margaret, looking exactly as I'd seen them on Nan's tea caddy in our kitchen!' Thousands of people poured into London to congregate at the gates of Buckingham Palace to see the Royals and Prime Minister Winston Churchill. Basil found the London crowds were jubilant: 'People everywhere dancing and singing in congas and groups trying to grab you to join them and dressed in Union Jack hats, waving flags, banging and blowing anything that would make a noise, dustbin lids, saucepans . . . Piccadilly Circus with the American Servicemen's Club at Rainbow Corner, jammed full with people, up lamp-posts, children on shoulders, American servicemen leaning out of club windows singing and shouting to the crowds.' The crowds were heaving at Buckingham Palace with everybody chanting for the King, and an enormous cheer erupted when the King and Queen stepped onto the Palace balcony. Frank was also in front of the Palace and he joined in the 'deafening roar of approval when they were joined by the Prime Minister Winston Churchill'. His mother had said to him, 'You will never see anything like this in the rest of your life.' And 'she was right!'

While the country was celebrating, not all of the people were. Vincent sat at home listening to the reports of festivities on the wireless, but his day was only memorable for the 'slightly disapproving feeling hovering over Grandma's comments about "people going to pubs and having too much to drink on a night like this"'. Some families were not celebrating at all because they were mourning. For them, VE Day was a poignant reminder of those they had lost. Fifteen-year-old Dorothy did not go to join in the festivities in London and there were no parties in her street. Her parents did not celebrate. To them, the war was not over yet, not with troops still fighting the Japanese in the Far East. Like many families, they had a son still fighting. He was 'serving on submarines and had not been heard of for months'. Shelagh's mother refused to allow any rejoicing in her family because 'the war in Japan was not over'. It was also Shelagh's brother's birthday: 'He had been killed in April 1942 – two weeks off his 21st birthday.' Marian in Scotland was torn between two conflicting emotions. On one hand there was 'this exciting and wonderful event' of the end of the war and she so wanted to join in the tremendous excitement and celebration, and yet she also felt 'desperately lost and sad'. Her mother hugged her, sobbing, as only one week before they had received the terrible news that Marian's father had been killed in Germany. Marian did not join in the celebrations: 'I didn't, I couldn't, but my memory of the conflict of feelings and being disloyal to my mother has remained a powerful and starkly clear image all these years.'

One little boy stared out of the window at the joyful crowd in the street below. He was another child who whom the advent of peace was a time of desperate sadness and loss. A few days ago he had found his mother crying her heart out in the bedroom with the dreaded telegram clutched in her hand. His father, like Marian's, was another casualty of the conquest of Germany. As he watched the crowd singing and shouting, he could not 'understand how they could be so happy and how I was so sad that my Daddy was not coming home'. Lorna, a student in Cardiff, had a great day celebrating but at the end of it she was silent. She could not help but notice that 'one door in that long street remained tightly closed'. In that house was a mother alone, cradling her baby. Her soldier husband would never return. Lorna cried 'bitter tears' for the lone woman and 'for all the others who would sit alone that VE night'.

Nine-year-old Yvonne and ten-year-old Alison were both upset about the end of the war, but for different reasons. Yvonne sat on the steps of her billet listening to the church bells ringing. For five years she had lived in the little village in Somerset as an evacuee and she had been very happy there. The prospect of returning to London was really upsetting and she 'bawled all day'. She did not want to leave the house she loved and go back to a home she could barely remember. All Alison had ever known was war, and the news that it was over meant big changes were on the horizon. This prospect of change was frightening and filled her with the fear of the unknown: 'Firstly, I didn't know what peace meant other than when it happened (IF it happened!) my father would come home and we could return to our original home, London, both of which were unknown quantities to me. I realized that other through letters and photos I had no idea of who my father was, what he was really like.'

Other children, including some parents, also did not welcome the end of war for the changes it would bring. Fifteen-year-old Harry in Kent had come to Britain at the start of the war on the *Kindertransport* from Germany and was in his school's ATC, eager to join up and do his bit; he had big plans and had been 'looking forward to get into the action', but now with the war being over he felt 'rather disappointed and cheated'. Britain was still at war with Japan, but he would have no Germans left to fight. Bill was another boy who, having joined the cadets and trained for the Forces, felt that 'for some of us, the war didn't last long enough'. Jean's parents also felt the loss of the war. The end of war meant the end of their wartime lifestyle and the purpose and identity it had given them. Her father unwillingly returned his 'stirrup pump, bucket and tin helmet back to ARP headquarters', and her mother was really unhappy as she had to finish her job at the munitions factory and was about to find the forthcoming 'lonely days at home rather tame'.

On 6 August 1945, an atomic bomb named 'Little Boy' was dropped on the Japanese city of Hiroshima, followed three days later by 'Fat Man' on Nagasaki. Japan surrendered and the war in the Pacific was over. In Britain, Edward's first inkling of what had happened was when he heard his father having a 'grave conversation with friends'. They were talking about the atomic bombs, something that Edward had not heard of before. The seriousness of the men left a deep impression on Edward: 'I have a clear memory on that sunny day of their solemn faces.'

Victory in Japan (VJ Day) was celebrated on 14 August with more street parties and rejoicing. VJ Day was something of 'an anti-climax' for Charles in London because the war with the Japanese 'had not had the same direct effect on us as had the war in Europe except, of course, those who had lost or still had relatives serving in the Far East'. The VJ parties in Southampton were subdued compared to VE Day: '. . . we did not go so mad. I think people had had enough by then. So that was it.' Though the celebrations were not as wild as those of VE Day, it was still a party for some and bonfires once more burnt holes in the tarmac of backstreets. Despite frequent attempts at resurfacing, Sedgemere Avenue in East Finchley still boasted the scar of a memorable VJ bonfire many years later. Vincent did not go out partying yet again. His family did however have a small homely celebration this time – a family trip to the fish and chip shop. Vincent ate his victory feast with relish at his Uncle and Auntie's house, and even had bottle of beer. A knock at the door heralded the arrival of another family member bearing yet more fish and chips: '. . . we considered that the circumstances were exceptional and we managed to eat the second lot of fish and chips too.' His grandmother, sedately sieving National Flour through yet another worn-out stocking, may even have approved.

Notes

Chapter 1: The Beginning
1. Terry.
2. Hansard HC Deb 27 April 1939 vol 346 c1300. The purchasing of German-made emergency equipment during the crisis and the subsequent outcry among air-raid wardens; Hansard HC Deb 20 July 1939 vol 350 c730W. The spectacular failure of an attempt to blackout the Midlands.
3. Hansard HC Deb 07 May 1940 vol 360 c1049. The dangers to dock workers of blacking-out the Port of Liverpool.
4. Levine, p. 240.
5. Hansard HC Deb 23 January 1940 vol 356 cc474–5. The advantage of Salford police force's uniform and lights in the blackout.
6. Hansard HC Deb 23 January 1940 vol 356 c479. The star-lighting experiment in London, far from being beneficial, actually increased the likelihood of road traffic accidents.
7. Thomas, p. 43.
8. Hansard HC Deb 23 January 1940 vol 356 c475. Road traffic accident figures in the first few months of war due to the blackout. The use of the description 'Home Front' was stated as being more than applicable considering the huge increase in casualties on the roads.
9. Hansard HC Deb 22 February 1945 vol 408 c1074. Comparing the figures for death by bombing with fatalities due to the blackout.

Chapter 2: Air-Raid shelters
1. Terry.
2. Hansard HC Deb 04 August 1939 vol 350 c2842W. Over 4,000 homes, usually those of the elderly and infirm, had to apply to the council to erect their Andersons. From 11 June it was an offence not to erect your Anderson correctly.
3. Hansard HC Deb 27 April 1939 vol 346 c1301. The cost and supply

blast-proofing above-ground Andersons would supposedly be met by local councils but was ultimately subject to financial constraints.

4. Bain, pp. 1–14.

5. Hansard HC Deb 11 June 1940 vol 361 cc1127–9. The scandal of Scunthorpe's unwanted Andersons.

6. Bain, p. 2.

7. Calder, p. 180. Also see Hansard HL Deb 17 June 1941 vol 119 cc417–42. The Lord Bishop of Birmingham and his condemnation of inadequate shelters including those built with no cement in the mortar. His claim that this was due to a 'cement ring' resulted in a successful libel suit being brought against him.

8. Levine, p. 62.

9. Hansard HL Deb 17 June 1941 vol 119 c420. The paucity of air-raid shelters made with lime mortar, quoting newspaper reports.

10. Hansard HL Deb 17 June 1941 vol 119 cc420–1. The demolition of unsafe brick shelters in Birmingham cathedral churchyard.

11. Bain, p. 3.

12. Hansard HC Deb 10 October 1940 vol 365 c528; HC Deb 08 October 1940 vol 356 c241. The disgrace of Glasgow's shelters.

13. Hansard HC Deb 06 October 1942 vol 383 c1064. Vandalism of Glasgow's shelters, equipment and water tanks blamed on children.

14. Bain, p. 12.

15. Longmate, p. 128. Number of Underground users.

16. Hansard HC Deb 22 January 1942 vol 377 cc440–1W. Figure for children under the age of fourteen sleeping in London's Tube shelters.

17. Clay. Details and history of London's deep-level shelters.

18. Clay. The clearing of the Tube at the end of the war.

19. Hansard HC Deb 08 October 1940 vol 365 cc351–2. MP Mr Gallacher's experience of the notorious Tilbury Tunnel in London.

20. Thomas, p. 70; Hansard HC Deb 20 November 1940 vol 117 c729. Recommendations for avoiding germs and infection in Tube stations.

Chapter 3: Evacuation

1. Hansard HC Deb 02 July 1940 vol 362 cc699–760. CORB categories and ambassadors, and an interesting comment by

Vicountess Astor that sending the orphans, the neglected and those in Approved Schools could 'wreck the whole thing'.

2. Hansard HC Deb 14 September 1939 vol 351 c 806. A case heard by the MP for South Hackney.

3. Hansard HC Deb 14 September 1939 vol 351 cc817–18, 822. MP Mr Buchanan angrily protested against slanderous allegations as to the condition of child evacuees from his constituency.

4. Hansard HC Deb 14 September 1939 vol 351 cc822–3. MP for Caernarvonshire on the unclean state of Liverpool children. One Welsh woman was fined £24 for refusing to take in an evacuee woman she deemed as verminous.

5. Hansard HC Deb 14 September 1939 vol 351 cc810–11. Scottish MP Mr Campbell on the treatment of the evacuees that arrived at Inverary. He also describes the selection process as being not unlike a slave market.

6. Malcolmson, p. 30.

7. Wheatcroft, pp. 127, 108–40.

8. Hansard HC Deb 14 September 1939 vol 351 c820. The unsuitability of sending Liverpool evacuees to a small Welsh village where there is no entertainment and only two pubs.

9. Hansard HC Deb 06 February 1945 vol 407 cc1935–6; Hansard HC Deb 15 February 1945 vol 408 cc381–5. The tragic case of evacuee boy Peter Baldock and his brother.

10. Wheatcroft, p.121.

11. Malcolmson, pp. 15–16.

Chapter 4: Invasion

1. Hansard HC Deb 30 May 1940 vol 361 c679W. Pony club patrol.

2. Crowdy, p. 77.

3. Oltermann. Ineptitude of German spies in Britain.

4. Hansard HC Deb 18 November 1946 vol 430 cc55–7W. German preparations for the invasion in 1940.

5. Finnis.

6. Hansard HC Deb 21 December 1944 vol 406 c1950. Eighty-nine POWS were recaptured.

7. Island Farm Prisoner of War Camp.
8. Bain, p. 15.

Chapter 5: Shortages
1. Hansard HC Deb 09 June 1944 vol 400 c1752. Comment about luxury feeding in restaurants.
2. Bain, p. 6.
3. Hansard HC Deb 09 April 1941 vol 370 cc1566–7. Regarding the carrot emergency reserve held by the Government.
4. Bain, p. 6.
5. HC Deb 28 January 1942 vol 377 c731W. Number of British Restaurants.
6. Women's Group on Public Welfare, p. 78
7. Wheatcroft, p. 52.
8. Hansard HC Deb 12 June 1945 vol 411 c1521. Comment in a debate of national health regarding immunisations.
9. Bain, p. 13.
10. Hansard HC Deb 01 August 1939 vol 350 c2236. MP for South Shields on the problem of constipated boys.

Chapter 6: Schools
1. Hansard HC Deb 07 September 1939 vol 351 cc561–2. Concern about London schoolchildren.
2. Gardiner, p. 21.
3. Inwood, p. 782.
4. Hansard HC Deb 05 March 1940 vol 358 c310. Regarding failure of the Board of Education to maintain the education system.
5. Woodard and Ross.
6. Hansard HC Deb 05 March 1940 vol 358 c312. Complaint about a school in a crypt.
7. Hansard HC Deb 10 October 1940 vol 365 c556. Sardonic remark about overheard suggestions on air-raid precautions in schools.
8. Hansard HC Deb 18 March 1943 vol 387 cc1306–8. Debate on pasteurisation of milk.

222222

222222

Chapter 7: Entertainment
1. Hansard HC Deb 27 November 1946 vol 430 cc1656–90. The dangerous effects of cinema clubs.
2. Hansard HC Deb 30 March 1944 vol 398 cc1531–2. Fatal accidents to children caused by explosives and the necessity of warnings in schools.

Chapter 8: War Effort
1. Larder.
2. Collins, p. 10.
3. Ibid, p. 3.
4. Hansard HL Deb 27 September 1939 vol 114 c1152. Debate on boys in the Civil Defence.
5. Hansard HC Deb12 October 1943 vol 392 cc728–9W. The issue of no provision of uniforms for Girls Corps was raised many times in the House of Commons to no effect.
6. Hampton, p. 102.

Chapter 9: Bombing
1. Hogan.
2. Bath Blitz Memorial Project.
3. Inwood, pp. 797–8.
4. Thomas, p. 76.
5. Levine, pp. 256–7.
6. HC Deb 09 July 1946 vol 425 cc352–62. 61. Court possession orders and chronic housing shortage. Also the homeless living in institutions, rest centres and air-raid shelters.

Chapter 10 The End
1. Hansard HC Deb 06 July 1944 vol 401 cc1322, 1327. Commons sitting on Flying Bomb Attacks.
2. Irene Bain.
3. Herbert-Davies; Maynard.
4. Longmate, p. 494.
5. Hansard HC Deb 11 November 1948 vol 457 cc1729–30. The case

of Barry Buller from Plymouth who was placed for adoption despite being reported missing.

6. Bain, p 15.

7. Hansard HC Deb 18 April 1946 vol 421 c2867. The reluctance to allow Victory bonfires in Lambeth after the damage caused in 1945.

Bibliography

Unpublished Sources

Herbert-Davies, Barbara, and Maynard, Margaret, for the history of their brother Sgt Douglas Davies of 218 Gold Coast Squadron. Correspondence to A. Herbert-Davies, 10 Oct 2014.

Larder, John, archivist at the Yorkshire Air Museum, Elvington, for his personal research into Air Cadet casualties in training during the Second World War; figures up-to-date at time of correspondence. Correspondence to A. Herbert-Davies, 15 Jul 2014,

Sources from the Second World War Experience Centre

I am grateful to the Second World War Experience Centre (SWWEC) for allowing me access to the archive collection of the Home Front; and for granting me permission to publish extracts. I also thank those individuals who donated their memoirs to SWWEC.

Andrews, Frank, *World War 2. Childhood Recollections of a Young Boy Living in West Sussex.*

Apple, Viv, *We Wanted a Lad for Our David. My Time as a Second-Best Evacuee.*

Aynsley, E., *A Child's Reminiscences.*

Banks, Thelma, *A Happy Childhood in Handsworth in the Thirties.*

Beedell, David, *My War Time Memories.*

Bennett, Jean, *An Account of a Child's Evacuation from London to the Country at the Outbreak of War.*

Berger, Elizabeth 'Betty', Letter to granddaughter.

Berger, R., *Granddad's Wartime Memories.*

Betts, William, correspondence to SWWEC, 17 Nov 2000.

Blurton, Thurza, *Some Memories of My War.*

Bones, John, *The War 1939-1945.*

Booth, Muriel, *Recollections of Schooldays and Evacuation in the Second World War 1939–1945.*

184

BIBLIOGRAPHY

Branwhite, Cleone, correspondence to SWWEC, 5 Nov 2002.

Brocks, David, *The Second World War Experience of David Philip Brocks*.

Brown, Muriel, *Gasmasks, Identity Discs & ARP Wardens* (held in U3A Genealogy Group file).

Buchanan, Frederick 'Fred', *On War and Peace. A Childhood Remembrance*.

Busbridge, Pamela, untitled memoir.

Butler, D., *My Memories of the 2nd World War*.

Calvert, Peter, *Peter W Calvert – Memories of Childhood*.

Cartner, Edward, *Edward Cartner's Childhood Memories of the Second World War when living at Morpeth & Whitley Bay, Northumberland*.

Cheves, Shirley, *Childhood in Lincoln 1939 – V.E. Day*.

Childs, Maureen, untitled memoir.

Chudley, R.F., *My Memoirs*.

Clark, Derek, SWWEC recorded interview, 29 Jun 2006.

Clarkson, Felicity, *Memories of Myself and my Family during the 39–45 War*.

Cleeve, Michael, *One Nation*.

Clutterbuck, Philip, *At War in a Police Station* (1939 – 1945).

Colbert, A.J., letter, 2005 (held in *Saga Magazine* files).

Colenso, Frank, *How I Became a Home Guard*.

Cooper, Adrian, untitled memoir.

Cooper, John, *Some Early Memories of the War, 1939-1942*.

Corry, William, *Memories of WWII*.

Cox, Naina, letter, 2004 (*Saga*).

Creese, Geoff, *Gunfire over Gordano – a Portishead War Diary*.

Dalton, G. Yvonne 'Yvonne', *War Memories*.

Daniels, Kathleen, correspondence to SWWEC, 12 Jan 2000.

Davies, Christine, *Golden Wartime Summers – A Paradox* (U3A Genealogy Group).

Davies, Margaret, *Memories of Doug and the War*.

Dicks, J.L., *Chapter 1. The Early Years and Evacuation*.

Downey, William, correspondence to SWWEC, 28 Oct 2000.

Draper, Laurence, *A Wartime Schoolboy's Memories*.

Duffty, Ida May, *Memories of World War 2*.

Dye, William, correspondence to SWWEC, 27 Jan 2002.

Eaton, Tony, *My Wartime Memories*.

Edison, Lawrence, *A Personal Account*.

Elce, Irene, *My memories of World War II*.

Evans, Marian, email, 12 Feb 2005 (*Saga*).

Farrand, Margaret, untitled memoir.

Feates, Frank, correspondence to SWWEC, 8 May 2008.

Fenn, Jean, *Memories of World War Two*.

Ferris, Brian, *Brian Ferris' War Memories: A War-time Childhood*.

Fiddimore, David, *Second World War Experience*.

Fookes, Gwyneth, *Childhood in Mossfield Road, Kings Heath from 1939*.

Forbat, John, *The Immigrant*.

Fowden, Margaret, *My Childhood Wartime Memories*.

French, Audrey, *Evacuation to Derbyshire, Through a Child's Eyes*, and *Audrey's War*.

Frost, Janet, *We Were Never Bored – A Wartime Childhood*.

Gale, Julie, *Memories of Wartime Childhood*.

Garman, B., warden's log books for Tilbury shelter, 1942 and 1944.

Garvey, Joyce, *Memories of Second World War*.

Gilbert, D.J.D., correspondence to SWWEC, 15 Dec 2000, and untitled memoir.

Gilbert, Olive, *How was World War Two for you Grandma?* and *War Time Food*.

Gilbey, Jill, *The War Years 1939 – 45*.

Goldfinch, Alan, *Second World War Experiences*.

Goodall, Henry Walter, self-recorded interview.

Goodbody, Mary Lou, *Wartime Reminiscences*.

Gough, Gillian, *My Experiences in the 1939 -1945 War – Aged 10-15 years*.

Grainger, Joan, *A Young Girl's Story, Sept 3rd 1939, My Small War Effort, Oh! Canada* and *The Night London Burned*.

Grant, Jean 'Sheena', *What did you do in the War Sheena?*.

BIBLIOGRAPHY

Green, M., *A Country Childhood in Wartime*.

Grice, Trevor, *The Evacuees in 1939 and Battle of Britain 1940*.

Hackett, Daphne, correspondence to SWWEC, 17 Jan 2001.

Hall, Alan, *An Evacuee's Tale*.

Halton, Ken, *My Second World War Experience*.

Hammerton, Roy, *Recollections of WW2 (and a bit more!)*.

Harding, Tony, untitled memoir.

Harris, Nigel, *Memories of WW2 in Caterham*.

Harrison, Vincent, *An extract from recollections of someone whose childhood, growing up in a mining village in County Durham, including the years of the Second World War*.

Hasler, Barbara, *My memories of WW2 in Crouch End*.

Hatherill, Ann, untitled memoir.

Hearing, Terry, *During the War*.

Heathcote, John, correspondence to SWWEC, 28 Dec 2000.

Heggie, Rosemarie, self-recorded interview.

Henson, Sylvia, *My Life Then and Now, My Mother, Christmas Day* and *Today's Living*.

Hickey, Jack, *My War*.

Hindle, Maurice, *Reminiscences of the 1940s* (in U3A Genealogy Group).

Hofman, Margaret, *London War Child – 1940*.

Holdom, Joan, untitled memoir.

Hooker, Ken, *Memories of My Boyhood (1939-1945)*.

Hoskin, Derek, untitled memoir.

Hughes, Edwin, *From an Evacuee: A Member of an English Family at War*.

Iredell, Denise, *A Teenager in World War II*.

James, Edward 'Jamie', *The Birthday Party*.

Jarvis, Alan, *Some Memories of World War Two*.

Jenkins, Harding, *World War II in Somerset*.

Jones, June, *The Shock of War*.

Jones, K., *My World War II*.

Jones, Phyllis 'Phyl', *Memories of an Evacuee of the Second World War – 1939-1945*.

Kay, Grace, wartime recollections taken from diaries written at that time.

Keates, Joy, untitled memoir.

Khan, Myfanwy, SWWEC recorded interview 23 May 2001.

Kierans, Yvonne, email, 31 Jan 2005 (*Saga*).

King, Jean, *My War and Afterwards*.

Kipling, Jane, *My World War II*.

Knopp, Dorothy, *Introduction, Masks, The Beginning, Strangers, The Blitzing of Bath, Aunts Help Out, Down in the Deep, Flying Bombs, The Final Day, A Royal Occasion*, and *The Display*.

Knowles, Evelyn, untitled memoir.

Lee, Michael, *The Day War Came Home*.

Leggatt, Iain, *Iain Leggatt's War 1939-1945: A chronicle of childhood memories of the Second World War in the County of Angus*.

Levey, Kitty, *Memories of an Evacuee to South Africa during the Second World War for my Grandchildren*.

Lewin, Harry, email, 25 Jan 2005 (*Saga*).

Lewis, Roger, *Some Impressions of Early Childhood*.

Linford, Brian, untitled memoir.

Lister, Reverend Gordon, *Memoirs of Childhood Spent in Wartime Yorkshire*.

MacLellan, Lady Jennifer, *A Child's War 1939-1945*.

March, Rita, letter, 20 Jan 2005 (*Saga*).

Marten, M.B.S., *My WW2 Memories*.

Marwick, Joyce, *A Journey to Remember*.

Matthews, W.T. 'Bill', *Bill's Story*.

McGill, Ron, *Brief Encounter and a Breach of Security!, Chiswick Incident* and *Sixty Years On*.

Melville, Shelagh, letter, 31 Jan 2005 (*Saga*).

Middleton, Terry, *An Account of WWII Evacuation Experiences between 1944 and 1945*.

Millard, Robert, self-recorded interview.

Moll, Eric, *1939, Going to Worcester, Evacuee 2, After Worcester, Shooting butts, 14-year-old and leaving school, The National Fire Service 6th June to March 1945* and *Army Days 1945 to 1948*.

BIBLIOGRAPHY

Montgomery, Robert , *Evacuees 1* and *Evacuees 2*.

Mould, Derrick, *Reflections of a Schoolboy 1939-1945* and letter, 15 Mar 2009.

Murch, Jill, *My War Years – 1939-1945 That Is!*.

Murfitt, W.C.R., letter, 14 Feb 2005 (*Saga*).

Murphy, Alison, letter, 5 Feb 2005 (*Saga*).

Napthine, Emily, *Memories of World War II*.

Needham, Robert 'Bob', *During the War, Trent had to be Seen to be Believed*.

Nellis, Mick, *Part 1: The First Seven Years of Men!* and *Part Two: Mick Nellis and My Life in Rodley – 1940*.

Newby, Frederick, *My Experiences Leading up to and During World War Two, Tyneside Defences and Battle of Britain*.

Newsome, Margaret, *My Childhood Memories of World War II*.

Newton, Madelaine, untitled memoir.

Nicholls, Jeff, correspondence to SWWEC, 24 Sep 2000.

Oakley, Pat, *Evacuation in World War Two* and *The Great Evacuation*.

Ollington, Robin, letter, 2005 (*Saga*).

Orchard, Derek, correspondence to SWWEC, 6 Jan 2003.

Otter, Reg, correspondence to SWWEC, 12 May 2006.

Overton, Frederick, *The Blitz* and *Birches Green 1940-1943*.

Pagden, Frank, *A Child's War: An Extract from the Unpublished Autobiography of Frank T. Pagden*.

Pageot, Henri, *Some Memories of WW2 Living in East Finchley, London*.

Palmer, R., letter, 8 Feb 2005 (*Saga*).

Parker, H., untitled memoir.

Parratt, Joan, untitled memoir.

Patey, Geoffrey, correspondence to SWWEC, 1 Oct 2002.

Paul, Susan, *That Strange Summer*.

Pearce, Clive, *Memories of the Second World War*.

Peart, R. 'Bob', *Post Office Boy Messengers of World War 2*.

Perry, Denis, *Boy Scout Blitz Volunteers*.

Phillis, Christine, untitled memoir.

Pincham, John, *A Grandpa's Story*.

Pope, Lorna, letter, 3 Feb 2005 (*Saga*).

Powles, 'Betty' Noreen, correspondence to SWWEC, 10 Nov 2002, including letter to student 28 Feb 1999.

Prentice, Bill, *WWII in Dunstable*.

Preston, Mary, 'Mary Preston', in *What we did in the War: Keighley Women of Today Recall their Wartime Experiences* (in Keighley Women file).

Price, David, *Blackout, Shelters, Scouting* and *Celebration* (U3A Genealogy).

Rawnsley, Margaret, *My Time in the Second World War*. Also Margaret's typed response to questions about wartime evacuees from primary school children.

Reeve, Richard, *I Was Home* and *Long Gone Days*.

Richardson, Colin, *How I helped with the downfall of Adolf Hitler*.

Riley, Brian, *Childhood in Liverpool during World War II*.

Rogers, Joy, *My War Time Memories*.

Ross, John, *The Secret Weapon Falls On London*.

Rudge, Maurice, *Life of a Ten-year-old Schoolboy during the Bombing of Bristol Aeroplane Works September 1940* and *Bombing of Bristol*.

Sanford, Peter, untitled memoir.

Scott, R.J., *Scott Free: World War II*, extract from R.J Scott's unpublished memoirs.

Searle, Martin, SWWEC recorded interview, Nov 2002.

Selley, Ronald, *Scouts Honour in War*.

Shoop, Stanley, *Highlights in the Life of Stanley Shoop*.

Shoulder, V., *Childhood Days in Wartime Years*.

Simmonds, D., *Memories of World War Two: Living as a Child in Hanger Lane, Ealing*.

Simon, Barbara, *A Child's View of the War*.

Simpson, Brian, correspondence to SWWEC, 8 Nov 2002, with subtitled sections 'The Outbreak of War', 'Leisure', 'Rationing', 'My Father and the Home Guard', 'My Days at Supermarine', and 'Conclusions'.

Sinnhuber, Audrey, *How the War Began for Me* and *Air Raids on Exeter: April and May 1942*.

Smart, Joy, *Memories of a Child in WWII*.

Smith, Charles, *WW2 Memorabilia*.

Smith, Eric, *A Child Evacuee in the North of England during the Second World War*.

Smythe, Ronald, *War Memories of a Child*.

Soare, E., correspondence to SWWEC, 1 Feb 2000 and 16 Feb 2000.

Stanton, J., untitled memoir.

Starling, Alan, SWWEC recorded interview, 4 Jun 2001.

Stephens, J., *Memories of World War II*.

Stopps, Basil, *A Childhood at War*.

Stranger, V., untitled memoir.

Sullivan, Edna, 'Edna Sullivan', in *What we did in the War: Keighley Women of Today Recall their Wartime Experiences* (Keighley Women).

Sutcliffe, Jill, *Wartime Memories, 1939-45 (and a little way beyond)*.

Swire, A., *War (1939-1945)*.

Tate, Ernest, SWWEC recorded interview, May 2005.

Taylor, Desmond, *Memories of the Second World War in Plymouth*.

Tempest, Eleanor, *Memories of World War II*.

Tomes, John, *What did you do in the War, Dad?*.

Trainor, Daniel, *World War Two Evacuations*.

Tyrrell, Charles, *Grandad's War*.

Veale, Jo, *I'm Going Home on Monday*.

Vernals, Dennis, *Beyond My Reach: The Story of my Life*.

West, Mavis, email, 27 Aug 2007 (*Saga*).

Wharfedale German Circle, *Teutonic Links*, a collection of research by Ian Andrew and Shirley Wise pertaining to Otley POW Camps 164 & 245. Includes: Recollections from G. Peacock, edited from two emails 25 May 2005, and Interview Notes – Gunter Reichel, 19 Mar 2005.

Wheeler, Nan, *Living Under a Cloud*.

Whiting, H., *World War II Gas Attack*.

Widger, Christine, *My Memories of World War 2*.

Williams, Donald, *Boyhood Recollections of Bedminster, Bristol, 1939-45*.

Williams, M.M.R., *Note on Wartime Experiences*.

Wilson, Jean, *Brief War Time Diary of Jean Wilson*.
Woledge, Julia, *Memories of War Time*.
Wright, Patricia, *My War Years*.
Youett, Myriam, *Some of my Memories of WW2*.

Published Sources

Anderson, Janice, *Children of the War Years: Childhood in Britain during 1939 to 1945* (n.p.: Omnipress, 2008).

Bain, Irene, 'Merton Historical Society Local History Note: I Remember – Childhood Memories of Wartime Mitcham by Irene Bain – 1993', in *Merton Historical Society* (Surrey: Merton Historical Society, 1994).

Bath Blitz Memorial Project, 'The Days That Followed: burying the dead', in *Bath Blitz Memorial Project*. http://wwwbathblitz.org./

Brown, Mike, *A Child's War: Growing Up on the Home Front* (Stroud: The History Press, 2000).

Calder, Angus, *The People's War: Britain 1939 – 1945* (London: Jonathan Cape Ltd, 1969; reissued Pimlico, 1992).

Campbell, Christy, *Target London: Under Attack from V-Weapons during WWII* (London: Little, Brown, 2012; reissued Abacus, 2013).

Clay, Robin, 'Deep level shelters in London'. Quoting Jackson, Alan A., 'Rails through the Clay', in *Subterranea Britannica*. http://www. subbrit. org.uk/rsg.

Collins, L.J., *Cadets and the War 1939-45* (Oldham: Jade Publishing Ltd, 2005).

Cooper, Nick, 'Analysis of Casualty & Fatality Figures', source: PRO HO 186/639 – Incident report from Civil Defence Region 5, Group 3 (City of London), in *The Underground at War*. http://www.nick cooper.org.uk/ subterra/lu.

Crowdy, Terry, *Deceiving Hitler: Double-Cross and Deception in World War II* (Oxford: Osprey Publishing, 2008).

Finnis, Peter, *Growing up in Hell Fire Corner 1939–1945* (Bournemouth: Cadet Technologies, n.d.).

Gardiner, Juliet, *Wartime: Britain 1939–1945* (London: Headline Book Publishing, 2004).

CHAPTER

_____, *The Children's War: The Second World War through the Eyes of the Children of Britain* (London: Portrait, 2005).

Goodman, Susan, *Children of War: The Second World War through the Eyes of a Generation* (London: John Murray, 2005).

Hallam, V.J., *Silent Valley at War: Life in the Derwent Valley 1939-1945* (Sheffield: Sheaf Publishing, 1990).

Hampton, Janie, *How the Girl Guides Won the War* (London: Harper Press, 2011).

Hansard Parliamentary Archives, *Sittings in the 20th Century (Hansard) – Hansard 1803-2005*. http://hansadrmillbanksystems. com/sittings/C20.

Hogan, Anthony, 'May Blitz Deaths (Liverpool)', in *Liverpool and Merseyside Remembered*. http://www.liverpoolrememberance. weebly.com/ may-blitz-deaths.html.

Hylton, Stuart, *The Darkest Hour: The hidden history of the Home Front 1939-1945* (Stroud: Sutton Publishing Limited, 2001).

Inwood, Stephen, *A History of London* (London: Macmillan, 1998).

Island Farm Prisoner of War Camp: 198 / Special Camp: XI Bridgend, South Wales. http://www.islandfarm.fsnet.co.uk.

Kidd, Ray, *Horizons: The History of the Air Cadets* (Barnsley: Pen and Sword Aviation, 2013).

Levine, Joshua, *The Secret History of the Blitz* (London: Simon & Schuster, 2015).

Longmate, Norman, *How We Lived Then: A History of Everyday Life during the Second World War* (London: Pimlico, 2002).

Malcolmson, Patricia and Robert, *Women at the Ready: The Remarkable Story of the Women's Voluntary Services on the Home Front* (London: Little, Brown, 2013).

Mayall, Berry and Morrow, Virginia, *Your Country Can Help You: English children's work during the Second World War* (London: Institute of Education, University of London, 2011).

MBI Publishing Company, ed. Perkins, Charles, *Children of the Storm: Childhood Memories of World War II* (Wisconsin: Wordwright Books, 1998).

Oltermann, Philip, 'Botched Nazi Spy mission was an act of

Sabotage', in *The Guardian*, 22 August 2014. http://www.the guardian.com/world.

Stranack, David, *Schools at War: A Story of Education, Evacuation and Endurance in the Second World War* (Chichester: Phillimore & Co. Ltd, 2005).

Terry, Gordon J., '1939-1945 The War Years as I Remember Them', in Scatchard, J.D. (ed.), *Spen Valley Historical Society Journal 2006* (Cleckheaton: Spen Valley Historical Society, 2006).

Thomas, Donald, *An Underground at War: Spivs, Deserters, Racketeers and Civilians in the Second World War* (London: John Murray, 2003).

War Department, Washington, D.C. 1942, *Historic Booklet Series: No.1: Welcome to Britain: A Guide to Great Britain for American Forces during World War Two* (Sevenoaks: Sabrestorm Publishing, n.d.)

Wheatcroft, Sue, *Worth Saving: Disabled Children during the Second World War* (Manchester: Manchester University Press, 2013).

Women's Group on Public Welfare (England), *Our Towns: A Close-up* ([London]: Oxford University Press, 1943).

Woodard, Geoff and Ross, Rosemary, 'Harpenden's Evacuation Scheme – WWII', in *Harpenden History*. http://www.harpenden-history.org.uk/page.

Young, Richard Anthony, *The Flying Bomb* (Shepperton: Ian Allan Ltd, 1978).

Index

5